TRIPPING INTO THE LIGHT

CHARLIE COLLINS

BALBOA.
PRESS
A DIVISION OF HAY HOUSE

Balboa Press books may be ordered through booksellers or by contacting:

Balboa Press
A Division of Hay House
1663 Liberty Drive
Bloomington, IN 47403
www.balboapress.com
1 (877) 407-4847

Because of the dynamic nature of the Internet, any web addresses or links contained in this book may have changed since publication and may no longer be valid. The views expressed in this work are solely those of the author and do not necessarily reflect the views of the publisher, and the publisher hereby disclaims any responsibility for them.

The author of this book does not dispense medical advice or prescribe the use of any technique as a form of treatment for physical, emotional, or medical problems without the advice of a physician, either directly or indirectly. The intent of the author is only to offer information of a general nature to help you in your quest for emotional and spiritual well-being. In the event you use any of the information in this book for yourself, which is your constitutional right, the author and the publisher assume no responsibility for your actions.

Any people depicted in stock imagery provided by Thinkstock are models, and such images are being used for illustrative purposes only.
Certain stock imagery © Thinkstock.

Printed in the United States of America.

ISBN: 978-1-4525-9147-6 (sc)
ISBN: 978-1-4525-9149-0 (hc)
ISBN: 978-1-4525-9148-3 (e)

Library of Congress Control Number: 2014901526

Balboa Press rev. date: 8/18/2014

ACKNOWLEDGEMENT

I'm eternally grateful to the many people who helped me along the way, and ultimately contributed to the publication of this book.

Thanks to the Balboa team for guiding me through the process that allowed me to share my story.

There would have been no book without Andre, whose tireless efforts made this all possible.

I'm grateful to Bill W., whose timeless principles allowed me and millions of others to build a foundation on which to reconstruct our lives.

Jimbo, my motorcycle buddy, thanks for offering me the opportunity of a lifetime and believing in me.

A heartfelt thank you to my lifelong friends Bill, David and Debbie for their contribution to this project and to my life.

There are no words for the depth of gratitude for my by siblings, Kathleen, Brenda, George, Kerry and Tricia and for my parents, Pat and George. Their unwavering support and unconditional love kept me afloat and gave me the courage to see each day through.

Most of all to my wife, Molly, and my two beautiful daughters, Cassidy and Kailey for standing by me in tough times and always seeing in me the things I was unable to see in myself. They were instrumental in allowing me to *trip into the light* and focus on a life with clear vision.

FOREWORD

All over the world people are striving to lead more fulfilled lives. Whether it's getting the big promotion and the payday that goes with it, becoming a better parent, husband or wife, buying the dream house, or writing a best selling novel, everybody wants to live their dream. And yet it's no secret that we live in a society where resignation, hopelessness and endless drudgery are the norm for far too many people.

So what is preventing so many people from living the lives they dream of? While there are many inner and outer barriers that need to be overcome to create the life of your dreams, perhaps the biggest challenge for the vast majority of people is their low self-esteem. In fact, recent research indicates that two out of three Americans have low self-esteem. Simply stated, most people just don't feel good about who they are and constantly churn in a world of negative self-talk. The beliefs that we should be taller, smarter, prettier, more athletic, and should have more money, lead to our concluding that we are not enough and our resenting the one person we should love unconditionally—our self.

As Charlie Collins so vividly articulates, these ideas are often born early and insidiously follow us into our adult lives. And, as *Tripping Into The Light* illustrates so poignantly, it isn't until we let go of these negative beliefs what we've been holding on to that we have the capacity to change and grow. Only then do we set ourselves up to uncover our true selves and reach our highest potential.

In *Tripping into the Light* Charlie Collins shares his personal journey out of the darkness of low self-esteem and self-hatred into the light of self-acceptance and self-transformation. While there are many individual pathways to success, there are two common denominators that must always be present—action and perseverance. You must continually take action, over and over again, and you must never, ever give up. Faced with seemingly insurmountable odds you'll see Charlie demonstrate these two principles with incredible strength and courage. His story gives all of us hope that it is never too late and never too dark to create the life of our dreams. It also reminds us that when we are ready, the universe awaits to assist us in the attainment of our birthright of happiness. It also shows us that by simply changing the way we think we can change our life for the better.

Often it is through the stories of others that we are able to find strength to carry on in our own lives. Charlie's story is such a story. Tripping Into The Light is a portrait of the human spirit at its best. It is a book-long chicken soup for the soul story that will inspire you to have the courage to identify and face your own demons and persevere until you overcome them.

Jack Canfield

Co-author of the *Chicken Soup for the Soul*® series
and *The Success Principles*™

INTRODUCTION

It takes a certain amount of audacity to believe one's life story could benefit someone else. It always seemed a bit narcissistic to even think such a thing—to consider my narrative contained magic; to believe that inside my adventure another soul might be touched, be healed, be encouraged to get up just one more time. For that reason, this book almost never happened. I couldn't imagine my life being a blessing to someone else; I was just a guy who never dreamed he would be the one that said, *I did it! Let me show you the way!*

When it was my turn to deliver a presentation in high school, I would quietly make my way to the teacher's desk and say, "Just give me an F, because I'm not doing it." It's hard to fathom the high school loser that I believed I was took the stage and spoke to hundreds at a Jack Canfield seminar. But I did.

The story I'm going to tell is about that road: the potholed, rocky, twisting, turning, cliffhanger climb to find my vocation as a helper. It was an odyssey admittedly made arduous by my own hand and by my unwillingness to look closely in the mirror and face fear. It is a roller-coaster tale of soaring successes and sinking failures. At twenty-six, I was a shareholder and vice president of a multimillion-dollar corporation with all the toys—jet skis, snowmobiles, motorcycles, and a beautiful home. Yet it wasn't long after that I slipped into a black pit of substance abuse, trying to medicate pain that money wouldn't numb. And then I rose again. And then I fell again. Along the way, I tried. Man, did I try. I intellectualized, calculated, cried, and made promises. I did all that I knew how and shoveled with the fervor of John Henry, but it was like pouring water through a sieve. The hole in my soul was not to be filled with simply trying, and I found no peace. I had temporary moments of reprieve, slices of joy that allowed me to believe my sun might one day shine—getting married, the birth of my two beautiful daughters—but for the most part I suffered inside a prison that I'd built.

Steven King once said, "You can approach the act of writing with nervousness, excitement, hopefulness, or even despair—the sense that you can never completely put on the page what's in your mind and heart. You can come to the act with your fists clenched and your eyes narrowed, ready to kick ass and take down names. You can come to it because you want a girl to marry you or because you want to change the world. Come to it any way but lightly. Let me say it again: you must not come lightly to the blank page." So I won't. I'm taking his advice and telling my story, warts and all; it's the uncut truth. And believe me, there is nothing I hate more than gratuitous stories of depravity, stretching the truth, or even telling lies to sell books. There seems to be running contests to see who can best alchemize their pain. That's not what this is.

This book is a way to say that I understand. My darkest moments are like your darkest moments. "Trust me. Hold my hand. I know the way." Not from an intellectual or esoteric perspective, but rather pragmatically because I've been there. I've been down in the dirt, stinking, foul, teetering on the brink of the abyss. Yet here I am, cleaned up and shiny, ready to tell you how I did it.

I don't have grand aspirations for this manuscript. I don't expect to sell millions of copies and be canonized in a Hollywood blockbuster. My dream is a little smaller. With every bump and every bruise, the pain that I've lived will be worth it if only one person's life is changed. That's it. I'm shooting for one person, and that's you. May your life be forever changed by taking this journey through my life. May it light a blind corner you were about to take with too much speed. May it encourage you to look at your emotional closet, open it up, and start cleaning with a new set of tools. Maybe you'll pass it along to a friend for whom you think it's perfect. Or, when you're done, you may send a blessing to whoever may find it and leave it somewhere conspicuous; airplane seat pockets are a great place! More than anything, I hope it offers you ideas on how to face your biggest adversary and in turn maximize your most valuable asset.

Fear is our biggest enemy by a country mile. We all have it; it seems to be the standard human condition. We're born happy, joyous, and free, but somewhere along the line, a vine of fear gets planted and creeps commensurately with our disappointments. Mine was so big it almost killed me a couple of times. But if you're willing to face it, it turns out it's nothing but a little purse dog that won't break the skin even if it did bite. I imagine you turning the last page and racing to the mirror to stare fear down like Dirty Harry.

I believe that once you've dissected your fear, a universal secret will be revealed to you just like it was to me. What's the big secret, you might ask? It's on you—the ball's in your court! It always has been, and it always will be. You will understand that you are infinitely more powerful than you've understood. You'll know that your rightful place is that of a creator. You will come to realize that your circumstances as they are today, no matter how dark, can be changed. I hope you'll see in the story of my struggles, in my journey from chains to freedom, that I'm just like you: a regular Joe whose life began to change on a chance e-mail.

All creators need tools. A carpenter creates with hammers, saws, and nails. A writer creates with dictionaries and lexicons. And likewise, I worked my way from darkness to light with a set of tools that I have included here in the text. They're yours free with the price of admission. Use all of them or use parts; personalize them the way you do your coffee or tea. But use them!

Henry David Thoreau said, "It's not what you look at that matters, it's what you see." This book deals with how we see. Audiences who haven't heard me speak usually chuckle and think they've wasted hard-earned money when I open with, "Did you know the number-one thing that limits a blind man from seeing is his vision?" Oh, how they laugh. But those laughs morph into inquisitive murmurs when I follow up with, "Did you know the number-one thing that limits a sighted man from seeing is his vision?"

That's what this book is ultimately about: vision. We may use our eyes, but we really see with our brains.

CHAPTER 1

I had no idea where I was.

It was like a movie, as I remember it. My eyes slowly opened into celestial, bright-white, and numbing silence. I would later learn morphine had a lot to do with the heavenly glow and thick fog clouding my mind. As I put the situation together one tick at a time from dreamland to the waking world, I realized there was someone standing over me. At this point, my synapses still weren't firing at full speed, and I thought it was a priest. But it couldn't be, so I squeezed my eyes shut, thinking he'd be gone when I looked again. I opened up slowly, peeking, and he was still there.

No way, I thought. *Please don't tell me I've died and gone to heaven.*

CHAPTER 2

Up until October 10, 1988, even though I'd earned the nickname Padre, I'd been anything but pious. A better description would have been hell-raiser, troublemaker, reckless, or even crazy. My life had been like a snowball of fear careening downhill and steadily picking up speed.

I don't remember exactly when fear attached itself and became my daily companion. What I do know is that as far back as I can remember, I'd always felt like something was wrong with me. I'd lived with a sense of impending doom, a dark cloud over my head. Many times I felt like I was born into a world that I wasn't good enough to live in. As my story moves on, you'll learn it was completely irrational, yet it was how I felt. I once asked my mother to speculate from where my fear may have come. She shrugged and said, "You were born with it."

She would know. There were six of us kids, and I was nothing like the rest. I was born at St. Mary's Hospital in Waterbury, Connecticut, on February 4, 1967, number five in the lineup. As my mother will jokingly tell you, "That one? Oh, he started giving me problems right from the start!" I was premature, just a little over five pounds, and suffered from pectus excavatum. In simple, everyday terms, I was early and underweight, and my chest was caved in, making breathing a struggle. However, after spending a week in intensive care, I finally made enough progress to go home. I had only been home a couple of days when one night I turned blue after breastfeeding. I was rushed to the hospital and back into intensive care. That night, a priest was called to baptize me because the doctors didn't think I would make it until morning. But I'm a survivor, as you're going to learn. I ended up staying in the hospital a couple of weeks, receiving round-the-clock care. Slowly I got better and stronger, and my breathing improved enough for me to go home. The doctor's parting wisdom to my mom was that my chest would take on a normal shape, but they weren't sure if I would ever breathe normally. As you might imagine, from that day forward my mom lived on pins and needles, watching me breathe. She's never said, but I'll bet those early episodes acted as warning signals of what was to come: I was not going to be an easy child to raise.

When I look back on my life, I often wonder whether those early episodes incubated the fear you're going to hear about in my story. Perhaps the struggle to breathe let loose a hormone that permeated my cells and hard-coded a story: that I really wasn't supposed to be alive.

Early on, however, you'd never suspect there was anything brewing inside of me. In fact, a single glance at photos of my younger years wouldn't suggest anything but pure joy and vibrancy. I was a blond, curly-haired kid who'd have given Shirley Temple a run for her money in the cute department. You'd think my life was one big smile. If you examined my family, you'd get instant thoughts of apple pie, red-checkered tablecloths, flags, and fireworks. We were the all-American, God-fearing, Irish Catholic family. Yours truly was even a smiling altar boy—always smiling, that was me. That was us: one big, happy family.

With all of us kids, each a little over a year apart, one can imagine what life must have been like for my parents. It was before the era of play-dates and minivans, soccer, and video games. It was just my mom and dad, surrounded by the raw energy of Trisha, George, Kathleen, Brenda, me, and Kerry. I'll say this early and often: my parents were amazing, and I don't know how they did it. I have two daughters, and between their talent shows, soccer, modeling classes, and parent-teacher conferences, I get lost. I couldn't imagine adding four more kids to the equation, but my parents pulled it off.

We were a close family, and I can vividly recall the joys of early childhood. The world was a giant playground, it seemed, and we were always on a new adventure. In the winter we took ski trips to Haystack Mountain. I learned to ski when I was five. Even though I loved ripping down the mountain full throttle, I must say my fondest memories are of summer vacation. It was pure excitement, piling in the station wagon and staring out the window as we drove from Cheshire to Hotchkiss Grove in Branford, Connecticut. We'd spend the entire summer there in a cottage, and it was fun, especially for me, because I loved boats. I'd spend hours on the water with my dad, the wind and bright sun washing over my face. It was during that time when I fell in love with the sensation of speed. Even now, as I think of those times, it makes me smile.

At the end of the summer, the Hotchkiss Grove community would have a celebration that was aptly named Hotchkiss Day. The event included a parade with costumes, swimming races, and a gigantic barbecue. I can almost smell the burgers and hot dogs smoking on oak coals. Children's laughter rang out as they played games of tag, beer cans popped, and seventies rock 'n' roll blasted—Bad Company, Eric Clapton, and the Grateful Dead. People from all over the region said farewell to summer and hello to fall, and they braced for those dreaded New England winters.

I imagine if you looked into your childhood, there would be some recollections that are brighter than others. Perhaps some played a part in shaping who you are; some may have given you a glimpse of the personality that would emerge. I have one such memory that I believe watered and fertilized the seeds of fear that were lying dormant. It happened near the end of one of our summer vacations. The remembrance is of me standing alone and staring wide-eyed at a motorcycle, wondering if I should touch it. Then over my shoulder, a deep, gravelly voice asked, "You like my bike?" I turned and looked at a pair of black leather boots, raising my gaze upward into the face of the tallest man I'd ever seen. He looked like he was twenty feet tall. I remember his scruffy beard, and he had ratty blond hair pulled into a ponytail that fell down his back. What struck me right away was how different he was from my dad. He wore Levi's and a T-shirt with a black vest, and he stood with a cool lean. He had swagger. He was bad—the good bad. All I'd ever seen my dad wear were shirts with collars and pleated chino shorts or slacks in muted colors.

"It's a hog." His deep voice vibrated my young bones. "A Harley Fatboy."

I think I turned back to the bike without saying anything. I was wondering how fast it would go and how soon I could get one. I calculated how many chores I would have to do to get a hundred dollars; I figured it couldn't cost much more than that.

"My friends and I are heading out on the water for a while," he said. "Would you watch my bike for me?" He patted the saddle and looked at me with a smile.

I lit up with warm feelings all over. The coolest man I'd ever met had just asked me to look after the most beautiful thing I'd ever seen. He thought I was important and good enough to do the job.

"Sure," I said bashfully.

And man did I watch it. I stood over that bike all day. I was not going to let that motorcycle out of my sight for one second. My mother called me to eat several times, and I wouldn't go; eating would mean I'd have to take my eye off the Harley, and I couldn't do that. What if something bad happened, and I wasn't there? She eventually sent my dad out, and I explained to him that the cool guy asked me to watch his motorcycle, adding that I'd eat later. He pleaded, but I wouldn't go. I stood there driving my mom nuts, and my eyes never left the Harley.

Finally, near sundown, I saw the cool dude swaggering my way. My heart raced, and butterflies buzzed in my tummy. Not only was he going to praise me for doing a good job, but he was going to take me for a ride. It was going to be the coolest thing ever! I figured I'd done exactly what he asked, not letting the Harley out of my sight for one second, that at least I deserved a ride.

He walked up and never even looked at me. If he made a sound, it was a grunt as he climbed on his bike and jumped down twice on the kick-starter. The bike roared like a lion shaking my young bones. He gunned the engine with me standing there waiting for him to say something. I'm sure my eyes were pleading, but he didn't say a word; he rode off leaving dust in my face.

Crestfallen, crushed, destroyed—I was all of that. My eight-year-old heart shattered like glass into a thousand pieces. *I didn't do a good enough job,* I thought. That must have been it. I was a loser and didn't watch his bike like I was supposed to. Otherwise he would have told me I did a good job and would've taken me for a ride.

If the hospital stay planted seeds that maybe I wasn't meant to be here, the cool dude episode was their germination… I believe shortly after that, a little green sprout that would grow into an mighty oak poked its head above ground. Soon after my life would start a downward spiral, confirming that God had created me as a loser and that I had no business here on earth.

CHAPTER 3

We moved from Waterbury to Cheshire when I was four years old. If you've ever seen *Mayberry R.F.D.*, you have an idea of what my town was like. It was idyllic and ultra safe, and everybody knew everybody. It was one of those places where one didn't need to lock the doors. Because if someone needed something, all he had to do was ask a neighbor. It was the kind of setting where car keys could be left in the ignition—a way of life that has sadly gone by the wayside. Even still, Cheshire remains a great place to raise a family with just a tad over thirty thousand in population. When I was born, it was a little under twenty thousand.

I had the stereotypical life of a small-town kid, and that meant chores. I had a never-ending list of tasks that I hated. The worst of the bunch were stacking firewood and mowing what seemed like football field upon football field of grass. If it wasn't that, my dad would find something for me to do. To me it appeared as if his only job was to keep yours truly busy. When he ran out of stuff, he'd revert to his default: "Is your room clean?"

This chore business was especially bothersome because my only real interest was playing with my buddies. I was the polar opposite of my brother George. This guy, to my utter amazement, actually kept his side of the room clean and would go looking for my dad for more work. I figured something was seriously wrong with him. Then after a while I realized he was doing it just to show off. I said to him a bunch of times, "You gotta stop, George. You're making me look bad."

He'd do stupid stuff like walk in the door after school and announce himself ready to do chores. *Oh my God*, I thought, *he is out of his mind.*

He's looking for work while I'm trying to slip in the door unnoticed. My goal was to ask if I could help just as everything was almost done.

Of course, I wasn't nearly as slick as I thought. My dad was wise to my antics and strategically picked his moments to drive home lessons… That's because I wasn't the kind of kid that one talked at—I was as strong willed and stubborn as the day is long—so he'd get me when I least expected it. One time I was charged with stacking the firewood. I don't recall where George was; I only remember being there alone and not being very happy about it. As usual, my mind was on my buddies. I was itching to be set free so that I could play. I slopped the pile together in a hurry and called my dad for inspection. He checked out my work as visions of running wild with my friends raced in my head. I thought he was about to let me out of jail when he pushed on the pile, and it rocked. I froze stiff as my heart suddenly raced. It was clear that if he pushed any harder, the stack was going to buckle. I stood there waiting while he ran his eyes over the stack. *Please don't do that again,* I thought. Sure enough, he shoved a little harder, and the wood tumbled like the walls of Jericho. I was steaming mad but didn't dare say anything; that would surely lead him to find more stuff for me to do.

He let the moment sink in before he said, "If you'd done it the way I taught you, that never would have happen." Then he turned and strolled away, never looking back. I imagine he was fighting off a laugh. "Call me when you're done," he said before walking in the house and closing the door behind him.

I stomped and mumbled curses under my breath. But guess what? I stacked that wood so tight that a hurricane couldn't blow it over. I still stack wood in the same way to this day. The lesson my dad quietly taught me was doing it right the first time.

When I wasn't working for my dad, the majority of my free time was spent hanging out with my buddy David, whom I am still very close with today. David and Bill, whom I met later in high school, are the true definition of a friend. They're still there after all these years—God bless them for that. There was a long period of time when I wasn't much fun to be around, but they stayed close and never gave up on me.

I met David in kindergarten, and our friendship was instant. The Green Hornet needed Kato, Batman needed Robin, and I needed David much more than he ever knew. We spent our time doing what boys do: having maximum fun. This was before minivans, soccer moms and organized playdates; ours was the era of sticks and rocks and bugs and imagination. We made it up as we went along. Our houses were on a dead-end road, and behind them was all we'd ever need: a thick forest of Douglas fir and blue spruce trees.

I've spent numerous hours looking at my childhood for signals, asking myself if there was something there that might have foretold of the trouble I would face. And believe it or not, those early days climbing trees with David were revealing. I've floated the idea that my early hospital stay might have had a profound effect on me; perhaps it initiated in my being the idea that I shouldn't be alive. None of this is science, of course, but indulge me for a moment. Let's just say the interaction with the biker, and his rejection, really did activate a dormant idea that I wasn't good enough to be alive. My natural inclination would then be to prove that I *was* good enough. This idea is the only one that I've come up with that explains why I was such a maniac from the get-go. I was on a quest to outdo anybody at everything, because when I did, this amazing thing happened: people would say, "Man, you are cool!" That seemed to soothe the ache already growing inside me.

If David climbed to a branch that was ten feet high, I had to climb not to the branch that was eleven feet high, but one that was twice as high. I was immune to danger. The fear of not being liked was stronger than the fear of being hurt. This would be the theme of my early years, and I'm paying for it today. Although I can't match Evel Knievel's broken-bone count, I'm up to ten, including my back. David was around for the majority of my crashes, like the time I fell out of the tree fort and broke my arm. Or the time I missed the bike ramp and broke my wrist.

David and I were pretty much inseparable. We even shared the same classroom up until the third grade, when my life took an unexpected twist.

CHAPTER 4

My brother George was about ten when he began to have serious problems with his eyes. He'd always worn glasses—the Coke-bottle thick, black-framed goofy ones that got him called "four eyes" or "Magoo." However, it'd gotten to the point where even the glasses weren't helping anymore. My parents took him from doctor to doctor, trying to figure out what the problem could be. They heard myopia, hyperopia, and astigmatism; at some point he ended up in a psychiatrist chair. As crazy as it may seem, the idea was floated that he had some kind of mental block that affected his vision.

While George was being probed and poked to figure out why his vision was so bad, my eyes were starting to quietly fail, but nobody noticed except me. I could feel something wasn't quite right, but I didn't have words for it. My mom tells a story of a conversation with my third-grade teacher, Mrs. Naples. She told her, "Mrs. Collins, Charlie is so restless. He's constantly getting up and going to the restroom. Then he'll walk up to the chalkboard and stare at it." She didn't know it was because I couldn't figure out why the words seemed to be fading away. I'll say this now for you to keep in the forefront of your thoughts as the story moves on. I fool a lot of people because I don't *look* blind. I'm not the image in your head of a man in dark sunglasses, tapping along with a cane; I don't have a guide dog. But if I had a broken leg or arm, you'd notice my cast. If I had a hearing problem, you'd likely notice my hearing aid. But tell me, how would you know if I was legally blind? Well, you wouldn't. However, if by reading my story you're able to gain knowledge and empathy, and then act accordingly, I will have achieved one of my goals. Most people think you can see or you can't, that someone is blind or sighted. That's not true.

Legal blindness, which has been described as a looming epidemic in many circles, is defined as a loss of visual acuity. What someone with normal vision can see at two hundred feet, someone who is legally blind should be able to see it at twenty feet—with corrective lenses. If the person can't, then he is deemed legally blind. In layman's terms, it means the doctor can't prescribe glasses strong enough to correct your vision. Why is this being talked about as epidemic? Because of the baby boomers and age-related retinal disorders. According to a University of Chicago study, Cost of Vision Problems[1], the numbers are staggering.

It's hard to describe the sensation of utter loneliness that began to engulf me at this point. The idea of being marooned on a desert island isn't strong enough. There were moments in the classroom when it felt as if someone had strapped a rocket to my back and shot me into outer space. I stood alone on Neptune, in the blackest black, not knowing how I got there or what to do next. And with the loneliness came ugly self-talk that I still fight today.

I was in the sixth grade, a time of tremendous brain development surpassed only by the birth-to-three-years period. It is characterized by an obsession with the opinions of peers, lack of interest in the opinions of parents, mood swings, tendencies to keep thoughts and feelings secret from parents, and an intense desire to fit in with a crowd. Sixth-graders feel awkward and desperately want to be liked.

So there I was, sitting in the front row. The teacher was writing on the board and going about her business, unaware that I couldn't see. The classroom was lively and filled with excitement; hands waved, waiting to answer questions in exchange for verbal praise. Some were so thrilled to know the answer that they spoke out of turn. And every time someone got it right, the teacher said, "Very good, Sally! Excellent, Kevin!" Everybody was in on the fun—except me.

---

[1] John Wittenborn & David Rein, *Cost of Vision Problems: The Economic Burden of Low Vision and Vision Loss in the United States,* (NORC at the University of Chicago, June 2013)

Not only was I not a part of the fun, but I was scared out of my mind. *What if she calls on me? I'll look stupid,* I thought. *I am stupid. I'm a loser. I'm the dumbest kid in the class, and everyone knows it. They all know I'm stupid.* That was what I thought on a good day. On the bad days, my heart beat so hard I thought it might explode in my chest. Fear would nearly choke the life out of me and leave my shirt stuck to my sweaty skin. As soon as she said, "Take out your textbooks; we are going to read aloud," I'd have to talk myself out of bolting for the door. Suddenly I had begun to have trouble making sense of the words on the page because they, too, were beginning to fade. This issue made reading a wearisome task. It took me forever to complete a single sentence.

That being said, it soon became common knowledge that I was "slow," as they politely called it back then. I publicly stumbled and tripped over easy words in front of the class, and the snickers pierced my skin like darts. *I'm slow,* I thought. *I guess I am stupid.*

For a while I tried to fake it. Panic-stricken, I'd calculate which sentences I would read and try to memorize them. I'd alternate counting the paragraphs and counting the kids, with the walls closing in on me fast. Early on, I was able to pull it off. I'd say the lines I'd memorized with a thespian quality, just as if I was reading. Even when it worked, I didn't find release because I knew I was faking, and I wouldn't be able to keep it up—eventually the whole world would know how stupid I was.

I have a vivid memory of being pulled out of class at one point by the school nurse. She wanted me to read letters off one of those vision charts. I sat down, scared out of my wits, and tried my best. I actually prayed not to be stupid so that I could read the letters like she asked. If I could somehow read those letters, she would think I was smart. But of course I couldn't. By this time I'd perfected the art of joking my way through pain and embarrassment. I don't recall what act I used on that day, but I do remember her saying, "Collins stop fooling around and read the letters."

Finally, after minutes of frustration on both our parts, she told one of her colleagues—right in front of me and with complete disregard for my self-esteem—"He's really slow." I put on my happy face and went back to class. From that point forward, I was banished to remedial classes.

CHAPTER 5

My parents took George to nearly every optometrist and ophthalmologist in town, trying to figure out what was happening with his vision. Nobody had a clue as to what was causing the problem. Ultimately, someone suggested they take George to Massachusetts Eye and Ear Infirmary. At that time, Massachusetts Eye and Ear was the preeminent research facility in the world. It was started in 1824 by two young eye surgeons named John Jeffries and Edward Reynolds, who established a charitable eye clinic in Boston. Soon they began to treat ear diseases as well, and by the end of the nineteenth century their small clinic had evolved into the Massachusetts Eye and Ear Infirmary, a nationally recognized specialty institution. In 1900 Dr. Frederick Verhoeff became Massachusetts Eye and Ear's first full-time researcher/pathologist, and he established the first eye pathology laboratory in the United States.

By the time we arrived in 1974, they'd been at it a while. Yes, I did say "we." At some point during the arranging of George's visit, it was decided the entire family should be examined, and so we set off on another adventure. We piled in the station wagon and headed to Boston. *Man oh man!* I thought. *A chance to get out of class!* For obvious reasons I'd grown to hate school by then.

We arrived in Boston the day before our appointments, and the trip got even better: the hotel had a pool! I couldn't believe my good fortune. There I was, doing backflips and swan dives off the diving board, while my friends were stuck in class reading. The joke was on them, and I couldn't wait to let them know.

Once we got to the clinic, the smile was erased so fast that it shocked my system. The situation wasn't a good match for my personality. I was ultra hyper, and of course doctors and hospitals and research are super slow. I had to sit for hours at a time with all sorts of electrical wires attached, and this cup-like device pressed hard over one eye. I was supposed to just sit there and not blink, because if I blinked it would ruin the test; that meant they had to start all over. It was torture. We must have restarted fifty times before they finally pulled out this cold, stainless steel contraption that forced my eye to stay open. It was not fun. After I was done with that part, the torture continued in the form of waiting. And waiting. And waiting. Remember, there were six of us, and everyone else was probably blinking and restarting like I did. We stayed at the clinic well into the evening.

During our first visit, the clinic discovered that four of us were affected with what they called juvenile macular degeneration. They didn't tell my parents right away, however. I'll share my thoughts on why I think they held off in a moment.

As it turned out, George, Brenda, Kerry, and I were affected with what is now called Stargardt disease. Stargardt disease, the most common form of inherited juvenile macular degeneration, was discovered in 1909 by Dr. Karl Stargardt, an ophthalmologist in Berlin. The progressive vision loss associated with Stargardt disease is caused by the death of photoreceptor cells in the central portion of the retina, called the macula. When you focus on something, you are using your macula. We use it to recognize faces, watch television, and read.

Stargardt is almost always inherited. It is inherited when both parents carry one gene for the disease paired with one normal gene. Each child has a 25 percent chance of inheriting two copies of the Stargardt gene, one from each parent, needed to cause the disorder. The parents are unaffected because they only have one copy of the gene.

As I mentioned, I believe the doctors at Massachusetts Eye and Ear knew what was going on after the first visit, but they didn't tell my parents. Why, you might ask? Imagine the exhilaration of the research team when we walked in the door. Four of six kids affected with a rare disorder, and they had a chance to study us? That had to be a researchers dream come true. We made semi-annual visits for about three years. The first year was on the clinicians' dime; they paid our travel, hotel, and food expenses. Year two moving forward, my parents footed the bill. No one had yet told them that there would be no cure. And believe me, they would have moved heaven and earth to find a fix.

I'm not bitter about what could be construed as deception on the part of the research team. I understand that not much was known about the causes of any retinal disorders back then, let alone those affecting children. Our family contributed to the discourse that has led the current knowledge base, and I'm proud of that. But maybe if they had said after the first visit, "Your eyes are never going to get better," I might not have fallen so far into despair. I assumed, as did the rest of the family, our visits would lead to a solution.

I lived four of the five stages of grief after our parents sat us down and delivered the cold hard truth about our eyes. In case you don't know, the five stages are denial, anger, bargaining, depression, and finally acceptance. It would be a long, long time before I would live number five and *accept* my vision disorder, as you'll learn soon enough. I was nine when I got the news, and for most of my life prior I lived somewhere in between anger and depression. I understood the visits to Massachusetts Eye and Ear meant something was clinically wrong with my eyes, but they were almighty doctors who were going to make everything okay. In a nine-year olds mind doctors are God and can fix anything. The truth of what lay ahead of me was confusing to say the least.

By that time I'd fallen deeply in love with motors. They fed into the obsession with speed I'd developed on the water with my dad. I'd dreamed that one day I was going to drive a car or a motorcycle, or even an airplane, and once I got behind the wheel, I was going to see just how fast the thing would go. Even to this day, the sound of a well-tuned motor excites me.

Once when I was seven or eight, I climbed under the hood of our tractor, found the throttle, and started gunning the motor. The sound it made as the revolutions climbed and fell was cello, violin, timpani, and crashing cymbals. I smile at the memory of my dad running across the yard and waving his arms for me to stop. I gunned it a few more times before he arrived and snatched me away. "What are you doing?" he yelled, out of breath.

I had it all figured out regarding what I was going to be. My first choice was Magnum PI. What could be better than a hot red Ferrari, a gun, and chicks? But if I decided not to be Magnum, then I'd be a jet fighter pilot; that seemed cool, too. And if I changed my mind on that, I'd just be a racecar driver. I'm sure you can see all three involved elements of speed.

So when my mom said, "Charlie, you have juvenile macular degeneration," I thought, *well, at least that explains why I'm a mental defect.* But I didn't grasp the implications until she said, "And that means you won't be able to get your license or drive a car."

Wait, hold up! What did you just say? That's how the words play in my head today. I don't remember exactly what I said, but I do remember the feeling of being crushed, like Christmas was canceled. If you've never had a dream snatched from under your nose, I imagine it's hard for you to understand. I can tell you pen and paper isn't the proper medium to express the hurt my tender heart had to absorb. It was like someone had plunged a knife deep in my chest. As far as I was concerned, my life was over; I didn't have a reason to live anymore. Live for what? I was stupid—the people at school had even said so. And now I'd never be able to drive a car? Life was not worth living, as far as I was concerned.

I hated those doctors. First of all, I didn't understand why they didn't tell us this sooner. Why did they keep my hopes up, keep me coming year after year? I thought the visits were about finding a pill or a set of glasses, maybe even a surgery, which would fix my eyes. "Nothing they can do," my mom had said.

Even though I got official notification from the state of Connecticut some weeks later, the day I became blind was the day I learned there was no fix for my disorder. In that moment, somewhere deep inside, I gave up hope and threw in the towel on a life I felt was not worth living.

CHAPTER 6

I was born in 1967 and took my first real drink in 1976. I say "real drink" because it wasn't the first time I'd had alcohol; I'd been sneaking swigs of my dad's Budweiser's for a while, thinking he didn't know. I'd carefully pop the top off a bottle, take a few sips, and then put it back in the fridge. Of course I didn't know beer went flat once it was opened, but in what became a reoccurring theme in my life, nobody really said anything. And when I did get caught red-handed with the bottle pressed to my lips, my parents laughed and said, "Oh, isn't he cute." I've wondered on more than one occasion what course my life might have taken had my parents reacted differently and sat me down to explain the potential dangers of alcohol. What if they'd helped me to understand that in my DNA, there was a history that could spell problems, even though I was just a kid? I don't ponder with regret but rather with simple curiosity. Over great distances, a one-degree shift in trajectory will land a spacecraft in completely different galaxy. With that in mind, then, it'd be highly probable you wouldn't be reading my story. I guess everything worked perfectly.

So like I said, by the time I took my first real drink, I already had a little experience. My memory of that day is as clear as if it had happened an hour ago.

There was great anticipation of the bicentennial year, and for good reason. When George Washington laid siege to Boston in 1775, fifty-two of his men were from Waterbury. Waterburians John Saxon and Mark Richards were with him at Valley Forge in 1777. All in all there were more than six hundred Waterburians who fought in the

Revolutionary War. Although we lived in Cheshire at the time, my family's roots were grounded in Waterbury, so naturally it was a big deal and the entire family was excited. To kick off the year of celebrations and remembrances, my parents threw a special New Year's Eve party.

I don't remember where my brother and sisters were. All I remember is being stuck upstairs in my parents' room watching television with Debbie, one of my childhood friends. I was bored out of my mind and antsy. I could hear the muffled sounds of music and the occasional laugh. It sounded like they were having fun, so I decided I'd go downstairs to see what was happening. My excuse was to fetch sodas for Debbie and me.

The energy of the party hit me as soon as I opened the door. It was clear that whatever was happening downstairs was way more interesting than watching television. I recall thinking as I descended the stairs, *I want to do whatever they're doing!*

While walking among my parent's friends, I could see something special was happening. If you've ever arrived in place where people are unencumbered and enjoying themselves, you understand: there is an unmistakable zest that goes along with those who are enthusiastically having fun. I noticed they were carefree with not a worry in the world. It was alluring, of course, because the unabashed pursuit of fun, anything to abate the gnawing inside, was what I'd learned to do well. I remember my parents and their friends standing in small groups and loving life. Heads tossed back in loud laughter, and every face seemed to have a gigantic smile that was a clear contrast to the way I felt. They were much happier than I was or could ever be.

I'm not sure how or why I associated the joy in the room with the martini and highball glasses, but it seemed to me that whatever they were drinking was responsible for the happiness. After I poured two cups of orange soda, I waited, and when nobody was looking I snatched a green bottle and ducked. I quickly unscrewed the cap and dumped heavy splashes of clear liquor into my cup. No one had noticed because they were too busy having fun. I put the bottle away and then quietly made my way through the party and headed back upstairs. I walked in the room and looked at Debbie, brimming with a slick smile.

"Guess what I did?" I said proudly.

"I don't know. What?" she replied.

"I poured something special in my cup. You want some?"

"What is it?"

I stuck it under her nose. "Smell."

Her eyes shot wide and she eased away, watching the cup like it was a rattlesnake. "Why did you do that?" She was horrified.

"I don't know. I just did," I said.

"You're not supposed to drink that."

Well that was all that I needed: somebody telling me I wasn't supposed to be doing something. I took a huge gulp and almost barfed. It tasted horrible! I later learned I'd poured myself a quarter cup of Tanqueray Gin. But since I'd started it, I finished it. I knocked down the rest in three chugs. It wasn't long before I noticed the warming feeling inside me. Then shortly after that, I noticed I didn't feel so bad anymore—I actually felt pretty good. Suddenly I was happy, and the night became fun. And so began my odyssey with addiction.

Yes, you did the math right. I got buzzed for the first time when I was nine years old. And as you may have already imagined, it was worst thing I could have done. It opened Pandora's box, and inside sat a perfect set of variables.

I lived in a state of constant fear that something was wrong with me–that I didn't belong.

I felt alone and was terrified that people thought I was stupid.

I'd already begun using high risk as my tool to get approval from my friends.

It was not a good thing to add alcohol to that equation. The ache that I felt in the middle of my chest, this sense of impending doom that followed me around—the gin magically made it go away. I didn't feel like a loser. I felt as best as I can describe, fearless and unchained. It gave me a sense of control. I had a way of taming the fear: it was in a bottle. This event led me to believe I could simply drink the pain away.

As my vision worsened, the walls of the prison stacked higher. And as my fear grew, so did the pain and the feeling that I was worthless. Fast-forward four years after that first drink, and my friends and I were guzzling Boone's Farm Strawberry Hill on the weekends. I'd hang around the liquor store on my bike and wait for *someone* cool to come out, and then I'd ask them to buy me a bottle. Nine times out of ten, I scored with no problem, and I'd pedal off to the woods where we drank. As outlandish as thirteen-year-old kids drinking wine on the weekends might seem, I can tell you that was the minor leagues. I hit the majors in Branford's Hotchkiss Grove the summer of that same year.

Branford's reputation as a summer hotspot began before the Civil War. For years vacationers had come by horse and wagon, train, trolley, automobile, or one of the several steamers that used to sail the coast between New York, New Haven, and the east shore.

In 1976, the crowd was what I would call eclectic. I would classify my grandparents on my dad's side and their friends as gentry. Two summer homes on the beach in any era means life is pretty good, if you ask me. Then there were people like my parents, who grew up in the 1950s, drove hot rods, went to sock hops, and maybe smoked cigarettes. There were bikers, a cadre of leftover hippies, and a ton of teenagers. I wouldn't describe the atmosphere as hedonistic, but enjoyment was high on everyone's list. For three of the heretofore-mentioned groups, that fun equaled drug use. Having older siblings put me right in the middle of a trickle-down effect. The teenagers hung out with the bikers and hippies, and I hung out with the teenagers. It was in that way I was introduced to smoking pot.

CHAPTER 7

If my early years were a television show, one might say it was the 1970s version of *Dennis the Menace*. Each day was an opportunity for a new adventure, which I seized and lived with passion. It was as if I couldn't live fast enough: I was in perpetual motion. It didn't matter if the sun was shining, pouring sheets of rain, or the ground was covered with New England snow, the disciples and I were up to something risky, and yours truly led the way, escalating the venture with the same certainly as taxes and death. Our activities often involved bikes and rickety homemade ramps with some kind of daredevil challenge that I'd thought up. We ran wild in the woods, built a tree house, and ripped around town on mopeds getting into mischief. With just a passing glance one would never guess that I was hurting, that brick by brick I was building a personal prison cell with negative self-talk.

All the Stargardt diagnosis did was confirm what everyone else already knew: I was a complete loser. I was less than, a mental defect. The official notification from the state confirming my legal blindness simply said to me, "Charlie is the stupidest person on Earth, and he'll never amount to crap." Even my teachers had said as much, right? I was depressed, possibly on a clinical level, and spiraling downward into a murky black labyrinth. That tiny spout of fear was now a vine crawling its way through my limbs. When the world was quiet—which I avoided like the plague—I wondered what I had to live for. What would I do with my lousy life? Everything I had dreamed of was no longer possible, and I was too stupid to learn anything. My friends would get their driver's licenses, go off to college, and make something of themselves. But not me. I was stuck, I was worthless.

I can't honestly say that at eleven years old I envisioned an act of suicide. I don't recall thinking, *I'm gonna slit my wrist or down a couple of bottles of aspirin*. But I can tell you with certainty that I wished I was dead.

Having said all that, I am a good actor. I'll bet there isn't a picture that exists of me showing anything other than my biggest, brightest smile. I could pop a smile on cue and seem perfectly happy. If you were to ask my mom about my life during that time, she would have said, "Oh, Charlie is very social." I had charismatic personality and don't recall ever having a moment alone. Today I realize it was because I was afraid.

I was the Padre, a nickname given to my by George, and my buddies David, Bill, Scott, and Robby were the disciples. All these years later they still call me Pad, by the way. I was that cool guy at school, the bad boy. I was not quite as shiny as the quarterback or the homecoming king, but I was not as sullied and outcast as the stoners; I was right in the middle. I was the kid your parents suspected was a bad influence, but they weren't quite sure because my acting job was so good. What strikes me most odd about my childhood is being admired and loved by so many, yet not loving myself. In my mind I was a loser, and nobody really likes a loser.

How, you might ask, could an eleven-year old fall into such negative self-talk? I have to say I don't quite know. But one thing's for sure: none of it came from my parents. Obviously they were thrust into uncharted waters. It had to be a shock, having four of their six children stricken with an eye disease they'd never even heard of—and one that was incurable and destined only to get worse. Although they've never said, there must have been a tinge of guilt knowing that they carried the genes. Nevertheless, they were suddenly forced to decide upon a philosophy on how we would be raised. I imagine the knee-jerk reaction may have been to coddle, to be our eyes as best they could, to protect us from all known and unknown dangers. I'm so grateful they chose not to do that, essentially defying doctors' orders in the process.

My mom talks of the day she sat with the specialist and got her marching orders, the dos and mostly don'ts of raising a child with juvenile macular degeneration. The doctor said at some point, "They shouldn't ski."

She shook her head and said, "Yes, Doctor. Uh-huh, yes, I see."

I don't think the door had closed all the way before the list was in a wad and properly dumped in the nearest trash receptacle. She's talked of many heartbreaks along the way, but she never wavered in her belief that we would not be treated differently. She knew that we'd be better off for the bumps and bruises. She tells a story of silently weeping while watching me play baseball. One of my friends yelled, "Jesus, Collins! What are you, blind?" sinking a dagger in her heart.

But other than not being able to catch a baseball because it was small, I actually excelled at sports. I even pole vaulted in high school. I wasn't any good, but it had nothing to do with my eyes; Superman's X-ray vision wouldn't have helped me with that one. I was pretty good at other stuff, however—frisbee, soccer, football, and hacky sack. It could be argued that I was among the best athletes in my group of friends. I figured I had to be the best, and my best had to be perfect. I thought it was the only way people would like me. It was a mix of sheer determination and coping mechanisms, akin to how I memorized sentences to appear as though I was normal. I learned to do things by feel. I used shadows and sound, and I had immaculate timing. I'm sure you've heard tales of a person gradually losing one sense as others grow stronger. I know of a thirteen-year-old boy who has been blind since birth, and he's never used a cane or a guide dog. He finds his way making clucking sounds as he walks. It's called echolocation, which is what bats use. Essentially, he sees with his ears.

As my eyes continued to fail, a complex set of emotions brewed inside me. The snowball of fear and self-hatred was gaining steam. I began to feel as though I was sinking. At the same time, however, I developed and polished uncanny motor skills that made me appear normal. Essentially, I was performing, putting on an act of outward cool and bravado. But deep down I knew it was a lie. And one day, if what the doctors said was true, my vision would be so bad that everyone would know. That thought tortured me, and my need to be liked soared. I badly needed people to tell me I was cool because it was medication for the pain.

I mentioned earlier that I'd figured out how to get people to like me, and one method was perfection. I was driven to do things perfectly. That quest exacerbated the negative self-talk even more. When I'd given all I had, done my absolute best, I told myself it wasn't good enough. I was always able to find fault in myself. Things that nobody even noticed, I picked apart with cruel self-talk.

The second tool I used to get praise was risk. Take my intense need to be liked and apply risk as the antidote, and guess what comes out the other side? Pure recklessness. I can't tell you how many times I crashed my bike by pushing the envelope. My buddy David says I was bold and fearless. As I look back today, I know that's not all true—in fact, it might be said that I was running on fear. I was so afraid that people wouldn't like me that I saw no choice but to make bold strikes to be noticed, to be liked, to not be a loser.

As far as I was concerned, I didn't have much choice. By and by, it became clear that my future wasn't so bright. At least, that was the way I saw it. My siblings' reactions, on the other hand, were vastly different from mine. Being declared legally blind meant I had free access to whatever I needed to make life easier. There were state counselors available to me who had been in my shoes and had made life work. They could help me choose the latest assistive technology to make life in the classroom easier—things like large-print books and pocket magnifiers. But there was no way I would ever use that stuff. Everyone already knew I was stupid. If they didn't know for sure, I was positive they'd heard rumors. There was no way in hell I would ever pull out a magnifier and give them the satisfaction of knowing I was a mental defect. And besides, I didn't see the value anyway; I was dumb and would never go to college. So I gave up on life and on school.

It's ironic that I thought of myself as stupid, but at the same time I was forming complex theories and playing scenarios forward into the future. I could see that my friends were heading off to college and I wasn't. I wasn't smart enough to go to college. That in itself was a blow, but it didn't hurt nearly as much as knowing they would one day get driver's licenses and I wouldn't.

Whenever there was stillness, these thoughts rushed over me in a wave of pain. I began to ask God why he hated me so much. Why would he take away all my dreams? I couldn't figure out why I was even alive. It would be some years later before I visualized an act of suicide. Even so, at eleven years old I knew I didn't want to live in so much pain. It hurt too badly.

CHAPTER 8

The iconic Henry Ford said, "If you think you can do a thing or think you can't do a thing, you're right." I love that quote; it ranks as one of my all time favorites. If forced to choose a single idea that readers should embrace by reading my story, this would be it: whatever you think is true. The concept is so simple that it appears like hocus-pocus when you first think about. It caused me to scratch my head and ponder the first time I heard it. But it is the absolute truth. We are what we think. I traveled an awfully rocky road before I finally came to embrace the idea. However, once it clicked my life changed almost instantly. Fortunately that moment wouldn't arrive until years, after I'd learned to self-medicate. Yes, I did say fortunate; it wasn't a misprint. You see, I've come to the conclusion that everything about my life worked perfectly. I needed to experience life as I did in order to reach a place of true authenticity, a place that allows me to share who I *was*, understanding that it helped me become who I *am*. Still, it wasn't easy.

By the time I was thirteen, I'd spent years indulging in the negative end of Henry Ford's equation. I was programming my brain with defeatist self-talk that would take some serious work to undo. I'd convinced myself that I wasn't very smart and would never amount to a hill of beans, and that made me an interesting social phenomenon in my small town as I moved into my high school years.

With authority figures—my parents, teachers, counselors, and soon the Cheshire police—I was the troubled adolescent having a hard go of it, the kid who'd been dealt a crappy hand and wasn't dealing with the news very well. Poor little, helpless Charlie. They felt sorry for me and, to my detriment, allowed me to live in a world where consequences were virtually nonexistent. In their defense, I would ask: How might you deal with someone who's thrown in the towel, with someone like me who just didn't care? I can tell you with certainty there's not a lot that can be done until that person is ready for change. And at thirteen, change was the furthest thing from my mind. I mean, change what? I was cursed and would let anyone who tried to come down on me know it. "You have no idea what I'm going through!" I'd often snap. I even told my mother once, "You had me! Just deal with it!"

With my crowd, however, I was far from helpless. I was a charismatic leader, a reckless wild man who could party with the best of them. I was fun to be around. But inside, I was scared out of my mind. It felt as if life was spinning faster and faster, out of control. I had no idea how anything would work in my favor. There's nothing more frightening than looking out into the future and seeing only storm clouds.

I'm sure there will be a number of people who knew me back then that will be shocked to learn I wasn't the confident, inhibition-free, swing-for-the-fence kind of guy I appeared to be. They'll be surprised to learn I was frightened of my future and was only putting on a good act. My shtick was to appear fearless; it was the only card I had. And that, of course, meant my eyes had to be a non-issue. I can't recall having one conversation about my vision with my friends during that time. I'm not even sure how they found out, but I know it wasn't from me. That would have required me to admit I was defective and needed help. I would never say that out loud.

With the disciples, I was light-years from needing help. I was the fun merchant, leading the way with ever increasing high-risk behavior. If they were leery, I'd entice them to take whatever leap I was taking. After introducing alcohol into our circle, the next thing that followed was marijuana. By the time we entered high school, my friends and I were drinking and smoking pot on a regular basis.

CHAPTER 9

I didn't know I had Stargardt disease when I guzzled the cup of gin at my parents' party. What I knew was that something was different about me. At school I couldn't see the letters on the chalkboard like the other kids. I stumbled and tripped over the words, making me the worst reader in my class. I was "slow" according to my teacher, and I'd been probed and poked by special doctors in Boston. When I got the official diagnosis in the sixth grade, it was a relief of sorts. As hope seeped away like a birthday balloon losing its helium, I remember thinking, *well, at least it explains why I'm so stupid.*

The diagnosis was as if I looked into a sea of circling sharks and was told, "Charlie, you're going to walk the plank." It lit a fuse of internal dynamics that, at a minimum, should have seen me enter psychological counseling. I was angry, sad, and worried, but most of all I couldn't understand why it had to be me. Why did God hate me so much? Our family was Catholic, and I was an altar boy, so I knew how God worked: he punished only those who sinned. I had to have done something wrong, but I had no idea what it was. It was a very difficult pill to swallow.

Not only was my family Catholic, but it was the seventies. The confluence of those two variables meant we didn't talk about feelings. What we did in our family was deal, so I didn't have anywhere safe to go with my troubles. My friends were out of the question because that would blow my cover. I certainly couldn't talk to my brother George; his eyes were worse than mine, and he seemed to be doing just fine. I'd watch him night after night knock out three hours of homework; he actually listened to my parents, seemingly going along as if nothing was really wrong. He wouldn't understand me.

Surely I couldn't talk to my parents because of the reasons already mentioned. Even if we did have a household where love and affection were openly expressed, I can't imagine I would have said anything. How could I? I had crazy thoughts of suicide swirling around in my head. In my eyes I was stuck and forced to navigate on my own. It was too much, and slowly my personality began to morph. By the time I hit high school, I'd gone from a happy three-year-old with blond curls whose genuine smile lit up the room to a surly, chip-on-the-shoulder teenager hell-bent on self-destruction.

Imagine a hypnotist. We've all witnessed their ability to plant ideas in a person's mind that influence behavior. The ideas can be completely ridiculous and irrational, yet under hypnosis they form that person's reality, and so they define what a person can and cannot do. You've probably seen the feather that weighs two tons and laughed. Well, if we were to peek inside our own heads, I'd bet there are lots of feathers to be found.

My ideas on life were constructed in a similar fashion to that of a hypnotist. I began to concoct Charlie's World of Falsehoods and carried a suitcase full of lies into adult life. The one I've struggled with the most, the one with the deepest roots, is asking for help. Somewhere along the line, I managed to convince myself that asking for help meant I was weak. The lie was based on unfounded fear and often led me to wallow in cycles of self-pity and resentment. I might have a desire or a need, but instead of asking for help, I expected people to read my mind and give me what I wanted, and when they didn't I sulked and grew resentful. As silly as it may sound, I took this behavior into my marriage. My wife, who is an angel by the way, married me knowing I was legally blind. Nevertheless, I'd sit around hoping she'd magically read my mind, and finally after fits of frustration, I'd ask for help. It is something that I deal with even today. But as I continue to work at getting better and developing my skill set, the time I spend wallowing seems to lessen. I owe a ton of gratitude to Jack Canfield, who wrote *Chicken Soup for the Soul*, for a defining moment in this area; I'll share the story a little later.

Taking in to account the psychological profile I just described, one might imagine what my high school years were like. I was driven by fear and was in all out rebellion. I drank and smoked pot regularly, broke weekend curfew, and went out on school nights. My side of the room looked like the aftermath of a tornado, and I skipped out on chores; the word "incorrigible" best describes my behavior. I turned my parents' lives upside down. I was utterly out of control and didn't care how I affected anyone. Maybe a better way might be to say, I was so sick I couldn't see how my behavior affected anyone else. I frustrated my poor father to no end. As I've told you, he came from the generation of hot rods, sock hops, cruising, and soda jerks. To him, I was like a visitor from another planet, a weird alien life form whose sole job was to break rules—with flare, I might add.

He'd often come upstairs to our room and find George studiously working on school projects. Me? I'd be kicked back on the bed plotting a way to get high, if I wasn't already. He would talk to me until he was blue in the face. Nothing worked. I'd sit and never utter a word while he pleaded for explanations. Obviously my silence frustrated him even more. After he'd leave, George would look at me with disgust and say, "I don't understand why you won't listen and do your homework. If you'd try just a little, he'd get off your back."

Do you think I cared? Not in the least. I didn't see a reason why I should even try. Life was over as far as I was concerned, and homework was waste of valuable time. I didn't see how it could help me in the pursuit of my two passions, partying and motorized vehicles; by that time my interest had boiled down to just those two things. And on more than one occasion I combined my two passions with disastrous results.

As rebellious as I was at home, I wasn't like that at school. Even though I loathed what school represented, I always went. Other than not doing my homework, I was the dream student. Looking back, I realized I didn't hate school because of the learning. As it turns out, I'm not the dummy I thought I was. I'm curious, a natural born engineer, and an entrepreneur. I was born with a knack for understanding how things work and coming up with ideas for improvement. There was a time when I took my motocross bike apart and had it in a thousand pieces on the basement floor. I showed George, and he just knew I'd screwed up big time. His jaw hit the floor when I put it back together and rode off popping wheelies.

He asked in amazement, "How do you know how to do that?"

"I don't know," I said. "I just know."

There was obvious intellect sitting there the whole time. I imagine the way schools work today, someone might have identified my learning style and encouraged me. But I grew up in the time of cookie-cutter, "one size fits all" education delivery, and I can tell you it was awful. My problem with school was that it was degrading, a daily reminder that I was a loser and that my life was going nowhere. Think about it: Outside the grounds of the schoolyard, my friends and I were inseparable, and I was a leader; they respected me. In our chosen fields of partying and reckless behavior, I made sure to set the bar as high as possible, so at a minimum I was their equal. But the moment we set foot on campus, we split up. They went to advanced classes to prepare for college, and I went to remedial class. This never sat well and represented a true conundrum.

I realize now if I would have asked for help—magnifiers and large print books—and put in the time, I could have excelled in college prep courses. But by that time I'd convinced myself I wasn't smart enough, so what was the use of trying? Besides, I could never let anyone see me use a device. They'd know for sure I was a weirdo.

So there I sat in remedial classes, sinking. I could see it wouldn't be long before my friends went off to college and left me behind. I told myself, *Even if you wanted to, you could never make it at a university— you're not smart enough.* Yet I felt a certain pressure brewing because by this time George and Brenda were away at college and doing well. My parents would be expecting me to do the same, and that was a scary thought. I had a brilliant idea to head off their expectations at the pass.

I vividly recall slinking into a counselor's office and plopping in his chair. I had my best "poor little Charlie" act going. My goal was to convince him I wasn't college material; I was there to literally talk my way out of college. I didn't think it would go well, but at least it was worth a try.

"I've been thinking," I said, layering my voice with sadness.

He was the stereotypical definition of counselor: tousled hair thinning hair, plump belly, only mildly interested in a loser like me. I'm sure I was interrupting the novel he was reading. He looked at me carefully and asked, "About what, Charlie?"

"Well... I, um, I've been thinking that I don't want to go to college. I don't think I'd do very well. The work could be too hard for me, especially with my vision being the way it is."

I was shocked when he said, "You know what? I think you're right. You're not college material." He went on to tell me why I was justified in thinking that way. Can you imagine that? Your child, at a crossroads, seeks help from a trusted advisor and gets the worst possible advice. That's exactly what happened, and I was happy about it. He verified what I already knew: I wasn't smart enough for college, so in my mind that meant I should ratchet up the partying. That's exactly what I did; I took my rebellion to another level.

I may have lived in a small town, but the partying was big. I'd see people snorting lines of cocaine, and we had our share of deadheads tripping on acid, but I wasn't there yet. At this point my world consisted of alcohol and marijuana. It was about this time when a new emotional pattern surfaced: anger.

Throughout my life, anger (which is the first cousin of fear) manifested in many forms. I could be apathetic, envious, standoffish, surly, or a bully; it would require a scientific study to understand the triggers for each version. However, when it first emerged, it showed up as wild aggression. The thing I was most angry about was not being able to drive. It was eating at me constantly because watching George was a preview of coming attractions. I saw how hurt he was by not being able to drive. He was devastated, so much so that he demanded my father take him down to the DMV so they could personally tell him he'd never drive; in essence, it killed the dream that every kid dreamed: the day when true independence arrived. That day when he'd stop having to ask our parents to take him places, and manhood showed up—none of that would happen for George. He wouldn't be getting a car like his friends, driving to school, and picking up his girlfriend for a date.

I could see what was coming. So what do you think I did about it? I started driving, of course.

My dad had a convertible, a 1971 Plymouth Barracuda, sitting in a separate garage. He'd driven the car off the showroom floor and well past 100,000 miles. His plan was to restore it to its original glory when he was done raising the last of the six kids. One night after having a few pops, I decided it would be a good idea to fire it up and take it for a ride. My parents were out of town, and I thought no one else would notice. I gave it a jump, dropped the top, and picked up my buddies for some joy riding. We rode around all night drinking in the car, with me behind the wheel.

There was another time I pulled out my dad's five-speed LeBaron and took off for my girlfriend's house on the other side of town. To this day I have no idea what this girl saw in me. She was a straight-A student on her way to the Ivy League, and she was gorgeous. What little homework I did turn in was because she would help me do it. It was well after midnight when I arrived, and the whole neighbored was sleeping, but I wanted her to see me driving. I wanted to look good to her, to show her that I wasn't a total loser. I roared onto her street and skidded to a stop in front of her house. I bumped the horn a couple of times while I spun the tires. The wheels were screaming, making enough noise to wake the dead. When I noticed the lights come on in her house, I jammed the accelerator to the floor and burned a trail of rubber and smoke. I sped home, put the car away, and didn't think my dad would notice. However, there were other times when the car wasn't so lucky.

One of those times happened with my sister's car. Once again I'd been drinking. I slipped into her room, quietly took her keys from her purse, and went out for a drive. I ended up in a parking lot doing doughnuts at high speed. I was having the time of my life, with the car spinning in tight circles and the tires squealing and smoking. Everything was going great until I hit a parking space divider. I hit it so hard that it blew the tire and mangled the axel; the force actually tweaked the frame. At that point the logical thing might have been to call my dad and tell him I'd messed up. But that's not what I did. I drove home on three wheels. The noise from the rim on the asphalt was horrific, but I just kept driving. I was about three blocks from home when I noticed sparks were flying from under the car. Somehow I managed to get the car back in the driveway unnoticed, put the key back in her purse, and went off to bed.

I remember being awakened by her scream. "Oh my God! What happened to my car?"

Before the fingers got pointed in my direction, I rushed outside and put on a good act. Of course I had no idea what might have happened and quickly suggested she'd had too much to drink herself and didn't remember driving. Because she never said anything, I was sick enough to believe she didn't know it was me. But she did—the whole family knew.

My dad didn't even give me a chance to lie. I was in the car with him later that day when he asked, "Okay, where'd it happen?"

All in all, during that period I think I wrecked at least three cars and totaled one.

CHAPTER 10

Closely related to my refusal to ask for help was a fierce independence. And that, interestingly enough, parlayed into a work ethic that saw me begin to earn my own money early in high school. Although it might appear out of character for the rebellious teenager who skipped out on chores, really it wasn't. If one thinks about my psychological profile, it will make sense.

It wasn't solely about work and its relationship to money—which I understood very well, realizing that if I wanted to buy things, I had to earn them. Work interplayed with the psychological fear that continued to grow inside of me. It gave me a sense of accomplishment and, in fleeting moments, the idea that I was worthy. I liked to work almost as much as I liked to party. That being said, a job well done served two very important purposes, which I'll explain in a moment. Before I do, however, I'd like to promote a gigantic pool of untapped talent to American corporations and small businesses.

According to estimates compiled by the American Foundation for the Blind in 2004, utilizing data collected from the National Health Interview Survey on Disability, a paltry 32 percent of legally blind individuals aged eighteen to sixty-nine years of age were employed.[2] I can't imagine there has been much change since then, and I think it is a shame. Think of how much ability is sitting around and eagerly

---

[2]   Employment Statistics for People Who are Blind or Visually Impaired:US, http://www.afb.org/section.aspx?FolderID=2&SectionID=7&DocumentID=1529

awaiting a chance. It wouldn't take much to unlock the potential, especially in urban centers where public transportation solves one of the major issues. If it's in your power, make it a point to hire someone with visual impairment. All it takes is simple, non-intrusive accommodations, which I'll talk about in an upcoming chapter. I'll bet you didn't know you've already invested in having them trained in the latest technology with your state and federal tax dollars. Why not bring them aboard? I'm confident you'll be pleasantly surprised at what you'll find.

Anyway, as I was saying, working met two very important needs connected to my esteem. The first and most obvious was related to earning power. The ability to earn made me feel good about myself. Research has demonstrated that our brain processes both social values and monetary gains in the reward center[3]. Besides that, I'd watched enough television to have fallen under the pop-culture spell that equated money with happiness. In the years that followed, I would try with all of my being to earn enough money to buy peace of mind, to make me feel good about myself. But early on, my needs were simple. Other than buying party essentials and a concert ticket here and there, I'd spend most of my money on motorcycle and scooter parts at a place that would later play a major role in my life, Willows Motor Sports.

The second and equally important byproduct of working was the "Attaboy!" My craving for reinforcement grew commensurately with the idea that I was a hopeless failure. Obviously I didn't understand the dynamics; all I knew was that when somebody told me I'd done a good job, it made me feel better, like I belonged in the world with everyone else. Sadly, however, the moments never lasted because as I had to do everything perfect. In my mind nothing I ever did was good enough. Perhaps you know this feeling, or maybe you know someone who thinks like I did. I'm telling you, it's a battle that can't be won. In fact, if not tamed, it will grow into a roaring monster that controls one's life. It became a major component in the vicious cycle that drove

---

[3]   National Institute for Physiological Sciences, news release, April 23, 2008; Cell Press, news release, April 23, 2008

me deep into addiction. It also played a role in keeping me there… Alex Lickerman, in a blog post titled, *Why Perfection Is the Enemy of Good*, said it this way:

"As long as I can remember, I've been burdened with a desire for perfection in all my creative endeavors. No new sentence can be written until the previous one is just right. No garment painted can be abandoned until its texture seems utterly real, as if touching it wouldn't yield the sensation of oil paint but of velvet, silk, or cotton. But my dogged pursuit of this verisimilitude has often proven itself to be the greatest obstacle to my achieving it."

Nevertheless, the above-mentioned variables drove me to work, and what emerged from the start was an entrepreneurial spirit. I started my first business as a freshman in high school, sealing driveways. I had a cart that I'd load up with three or four pails of sealer, a hand blower, and a squeegee. I'd hold the cart with one hand and drive my scooter with the other on the hunt for jobs. It was old-school, door-to-door sales at first, but soon I would learn a valuable lesson that I still value today. I learned that a job well done would cause people to talk. It wasn't long before homeowners were looking for me. I saved them money and did a fantastic job. It'd take me half a day to knock out a couple of driveways at 160 bucks a pop, and then I'd be on my way to buy beer and hit up a party.

It wasn't until the summer of my sophomore year that I got my first real job working at the Copper Valley Swim and Tennis Club. I don't remember exactly how I talked my way into the job, but I do recall never mentioning that I had a visual impairment. I was certain that if they knew, they'd never hire me. I mean, who would want a visually impaired loser looking after their tennis courts? So I kept quiet and went about my business, hiding my impairment like I'd always done and never once asking for help. I turned out to be really good at the job. I maintained eight tennis courts and kept them in pristine condition.

My vision deteriorated on a slow, steady continuum. As a frame of reference, here are some numbers: In 1980 I was deemed legally blind by the State of Connecticut with visual acuity of 20/200. (I still have the letter, by the way.) There was also impaired color vision in the red-green range, which my siblings and I shared. George, who was about five years older, was 20/300 in both eyes at that time. I got the job at the tennis club in 1983, three years after my official diagnosis. As you can gather, using George's acuity as a loose gauge, my vision had significantly declined by then. It has continued downhill—today my acuity is 20/400 at best.

As my eyes failed, I continued to develop ways to get things done. I believe it went back to my mother's idea that we would be treated like normal sighted children. I didn't know the doctors had told her I shouldn't ski, so I did. I had no idea I wasn't supposed to be able to catch Frisbees, so I did. Nobody ever told me I couldn't maintain tennis courts, so I did. I remember vividly the day word got out that I had vision impairment. I was scared to death they were going to fire me. Instead, one of the supervisors sat me down and wanted to know how on earth I was able to do my job. All I managed was a shrug. I didn't have a good answer because I'd never given it a second thought; I just did things. To work on the courts, for instance, I would use shadows. First I'd sweep one direction, creating a different shade on the court. While coming back the other direction, I'd match the shades and go back and forth until the court was uniform. Then, underneath the shade I was able to see the faint white line that I swept with a rotating broom. Bingo! The best-looking tennis courts in the state. And they had to be that way. Everything I did had to be perfect.

I worked at the country club for the remainder of my high school years. The convergence of the variables I've mentioned—fierce independence, earning power, praise, the work ethic my father instilled—came into play. The club members liked having me around because I kept the courts in immaculate condition. My boss liked me because I worked my tail off. It was a good place, and I was comfortable—clearly a stark contrast to the feeling I got at school and the potential horror of college hanging over my head.

I'm not sure what day it happened, but at some point I figured I'd settled into my future, or at least some version of it. I'd get a job after high school, work hard during the day, and party at night, just like I was already doing.

Well, I was wrong. I ended up giving college a try—well, actually, *several* unsuccessful tries.

CHAPTER 11

I did everything in my power to avoid college. On top of that visit to the counselor's office, I didn't take a single college prep course. My grades were horrible, even in remedial classes. And when it came to the SAT, all I did was color the dots in a cool pattern. However, in spite of the passive-aggressive moves to ruin my chances, I applied to Central Connecticut State University (CCSU) and somehow got in. I couldn't believe it when the acceptance letter came. I'd thought for sure they'd never let a loser like me into college, but they did—with a probationary restriction that I couldn't live on campus right away. I would have to commute.

All those years I'd dreaded the thought of college, and here I was about to enter my worst nightmare. I'd only enrolled because that's what I was supposed to do. All my friends had done it, gotten accepted, and were excited about going away. Tricia and George had already graduated, and Kathleen was on deck. I caved under the pressure, and the weight overwhelmed me. The truth was I'd been such a screw-up that I didn't have the courage to tell my parents I wasn't going to college. I was already the black sheep, and that would be the act that labeled me a complete and utter failure. I thought I had to at least pretend for a little while.

CCSU was about a half hour from our house. Every morning my dad would faithfully drive me to the entrance, drop me off, and pick me up at the day's end. The ride slowly grew into a torture session. Every day was going to be the day that I told him college wasn't for me, that I wasn't smart enough to make it. But somehow I could never quite get the words out, so I came up with another plan. I decided to just sit in class and do nothing until they kicked me out. It turned out I was too unhappy to do even that.

In my mind classrooms were very bad places. They were closer to a circus funhouse of murderous clowns than they were to a safe place of learning. The only experiences I could recall in classrooms were bad ones. As far as I was concerned, it was impossible that this situation would be any different. And it wasn't. I remember walking into a lecture and instantly wishing I was invisible. The panicked feeling I felt in third grade blew over me like storm winds and choked off my breath. It was the exact same nervousness that surfaced when it was time to read aloud. As I slunk to the front of the room with my eyes on the floor, it felt like 150 laser-hot eyeballs gouging into my flesh. I took my seat and sat paralyzed by fear for the entire hour. I knew everyone was thinking about me and how stupid I was. I thought I was going to have a breakdown that day.

It was maybe two months in when the anxiety of trying to fake it boiled over. I came home one night after having too much to drink, and it spilled in a tear-filled, raging emotional fit. I told my parents I hated college. I hated life. I hated myself, and if I had to go back, I'd rather kill myself. And that time I was serious.

By that time thoughts of suicide were with me wherever I went. Not yet a willingness to stick a pistol in my mouth or anything like that— rather it had become a serious questioning of reasons to live. Lurking just off my shoulder and waiting for a moment of quiet sobriety was a voice that said, *You're a loser, Charlie. You may as well be dead.*

My waking hours became a fight to keep that voice at bay, and inebriation was my main tool. In fact, it was the only one in the box. I lived life with the volume on ten, full speed ahead, raging and in all out party mode. It was all I could do to quiet the voices and this sense of impending doom. Even still, in the midst of drunkenness and surrounded by friends, there would be moments when despair would engulf me.

There is a story my friends tell of when it hit home that something was seriously wrong. We were at a party, and I'd had quite a bit to drink, so I don't remember the details. But as the story goes, they could tell that something was off that night; I was extra melancholy. They were used to me cycling in and out the various faces of anger that I described earlier, so my emotional swings weren't all that usual. But typically I got up for parties: after a couple of beers and a couple of shots of Cuervo, I was good time Charlie. But not that night. They said at some point I began giving stuff away—my wallet, my keys, and my prized watch. Apparently I even gave instructions on what to tell my girlfriend, because "I'm going away."

And then I vanished.

I imagine that had my behavior not been so bizarre, they would have kept right on partying. But collectively they decided to come find me, just to make sure I was okay. Well, I wasn't. Someone—I don't remember who—apparently found me lying prone in the middle of one of the town's busiest intersections.

I'm sure that raised all sorts of red flags, right? And it should. It was a classic cry for help, but nobody heard me. I woke up the next day, laughed it off, and kept right on marching.

Needless to say, my parents were shocked by the revelation of how much I hated college life. They had no idea of the true emotion that was churning inside of me. They knew I was troubled, yes, but they didn't have a clue just how much danger I was in. Nobody did.

We sat and talked about my life and, for the first time that I could remember, my emotions. Turns out college wasn't the requirement that I'd made it out to be. It was, is, and will always be their desire for me to live a balanced life that makes *me* happy. So they accepted my wishes, and we agreed that I would not go back to CCSU. However, the deal was that I would get a job and pay rent, and that's what I did … for awhile. Believe it or not, I actually tried college two more times, of my own volition. Oh yes, there came a time when I realized a college campus was the place where all my dreams could be fulfilled.

I'd gone to visit one of my buddies who was going to school in Vermont. I happened to stay in his dorm room over the weekend, and holy smokes! Somehow I'd missed very critical information during my two months at CCSU: the best parties in the world happened on college campuses. It was the perfect set up. There were kegs of beer, plenty of marijuana, plus access to any other substance I might want. And chicks—hot chicks were all over the place. What more could I ask for? I went on a drunken tear that weekend, so much so that I was escorted off campus, and it was strongly suggested that I never return.

Certain I'd found my calling, though. I went home and told my parents I needed to find a college immediately.

"What did you say?" my mom asked, raising her brow.

"I want to give college one more try," I said.

I finished up with a very convincing story about how it would make me a better person. It was baloney of course, but I sold them on the idea. They were shocked at the turnaround, but nevertheless happy to see I was taking steps to get my life together.

Obviously my premise had nothing to do with learning, so I didn't last the semester. I showed up to my dorm room and set up my stereo right away. Next I found out the closest place to score party essentials, and then it was on. For six to eight weeks I was an absolute wild man. I was either at a party, hung over from one, or hosting my own. After about a week, my dorm room was known as party central. I'd open my door and crank some Grateful Dead, and like magic the beer began to flow, coeds showed up, and the fun started. I don't think I made it to more than the first week of classes. I partied nonstop until they asked me to leave.

Then I went back home and worked until the college bug bit me again.

I didn't realize my dad was putting the rent money I paid into a savings account, so when I went to him and said, "Dad I'm ready to try a college again," he suggested it was time to spend my own money.

I still see his face in my mind's eye and smile, thinking about what he said. In the middle of signing the check, he paused, lifted his pen, and took me in. His head was tilted just a little, and he had a rather serious look on his face. I was expecting paternal words of encouragement—something like, "You can do it, Charlie," or maybe, "I'm behind you 100 percent, son. I'm here if you need me; just call." Instead, with not even a hint of a smile, he asked, "Why don't you just take a cruise?"

Can you believe I was actually offended? Or at least I pretended to be. I think I said something like, "Dad, I can't believe you just said that! This time I'm serious. I'm going to make it work."

I actually had good intentions—sort of. I mean, I did have to work to get accepted, and I'd done that all on my own. Before they let me in, I was required to have a face-to-face with the dean. Because believe it or not, I was going back to my buddies college in Vermont! Yep, that's right—I was heading back to the scene of the crime.

As you've probably guessed, it was a repeat performance, and I was back home in six weeks and this time done with college for good. I quickly fell into a mundane "work hard, party harder" routine that I thought would be the story of my life.

CHAPTER 12

I was living at home with my parents and going through the motions. During the summer I worked for a company that built tennis courts. My experience at Copper Valley came in handy and it wasn't long before I became a foreman. I'll tell you more about that in a moment, but first I want to fill you in on my winter job at a local ski shop. As it turned out that job would play a major role in my future success. First, the retail experience was the perfect training ground for the next two companies I would manage. Second, and most importantly, it's where I saw my wife for the first time. I walked into work and there she was. Perfect as could be. I had one of those moments where the clocks stop ticking and world retreats into hushed-silence. *Oh my God... She's beautiful...* I thought.

It wasn't actually the first time I'd seen her but rather the first time I *saw* her, if you know what I'm saying? In truth I'd met her way back in 7th grade at a backyard pool party. She was lanky, pretty and blonde with a mouth full of braces. And, just as she is today, sweet as can be. You've already gathered sweet is not a word best used to describe who I was back then. I had my mind on weed, cigarettes, beer, and seeing how much hell I could raise. Needless to say I wasn't interested in anything sweet at the time. Our paths crossed now-and-then during high school. I might see her at a party or catch her on the porch as I ripped down her street on my moped. I recall once she gave me and my buddies bubble gum when we stopped to say hi. But, you know, I wasn't paying attention to her. Besides, I had a girlfriend and she had a boyfriend.

All that changed, big time, the day I showed up for work at the ski shop. She was home for winter break from her freshman year in college.

The braces were long-gone and before me stood the most beautiful woman I had ever seen. Besides the physical allure she had a quiet strength that drew me in. I didn't understand how just rock-solid she really was, of course. And how her sturdiness would reveal itself over the course of our relationship—that she would end up being an anchor while my life spun out of control. All I knew was I needed to have her in my life. In that moment I embarked on what would be a two-year sales pitch of rising intensity to get her to dump the boyfriend. After that first year of working together I realized I was hooked. The following year as winter approached, I recall daydreaming, wondering when would she be back in town so I could continue selling her my virtues. It made going to work the highlight of my day. Seriously, I couldn't wait to get there. I got to see Molly and on top of that I was killing it on the sales floor.

Keep in mind that as we move forward, the turmoil continued to percolate underneath the surface. I still hadn't come to grips with my vision disorder. The result of that complicated emotional cocktail was a steady fear-induced inebriation. I earnestly began to question my very existence as I looked into a future that I considered a dead end. It was about this time I began to seriously ask, *is this the life you're supposed to be living? Really, Charlie? This can't be all that there is... because this is not any fun...*

In the meantime, however, life is *looking* pretty good. From the outside at least. My brother George had graduated from college by then and just so happened to be the store manager—and my boss. Of course he's the one that got me the job and the situation was as good as it could get. I'm working for my older brother, with friends I'd known since grade school, and the woman I would end up marrying. We were a close group that worked hard and played even harder, though nobody went after it as hard as I did. Admittedly, big brother had to cover for me more than once after a night of debauchery. Even still, I was great at selling anything having to do with ski's... I brought enthusiasm to the job and, even as I suffered emotionally, a heartfelt desire to help people. I'd skied for years, thanks to my mom disobeying the doctors' orders, so I knew the business from the perspective of the user. This theme became a common thread as my career evolved. I inevitably ended up selling products with which I had personal, practical experience.

To compensate for my vision, which had deteriorated further, I simply memorized the entire store top to bottom. No pun intended, I could do the job blind. I knew where every item was located, and I remembered obscure part numbers and rattled them off with ease. Instead of hunting in manuals, my coworkers would ask me questions. I'd memorized the register strokes and didn't need to use what little eyesight I had. Month after month, winter after winter, I was the top salesperson and made good money. In fits and starts, I even managed to stay sober, but it never lasted.

Because the disciples were away at college, I'd fallen in with a new group of friends, and let's just say they were unsavory. George took one look at them and shook his head. "What a bunch of losers," he said. By hanging out with those guys, my life eventually turned into what seemed like a never-ending party. It was the mid-eighties, and suddenly powdered cocaine seemed to fall out of sky. One day I'd never heard of it, and the next people were doing lines everywhere I turned. I don't recall who introduced it to me and my circle of friends, but it took off like wildfire and yours truly became a casual user. It made me feel good and calmed the emotional hurricane brewing inside. Let's not forget that before anyone figured out how destructive it was, cocaine was lauded as a wonder drug and was sold as a cure-all. It was promoted by some of the greatest minds in medical history, including Sigmund Freud and the pioneering surgeon William Halsted.

However, nothing—not alcohol, cocaine, my so-called success, money, accolades of being the top salesman, or a budding relationship with my future wife—stemmed the tide of fear for very long. It was always there, the gnawing in my mind that had been planted early on that I wasn't good enough. It seemed to entrench me in a duality that's difficult to describe. On the one hand, it drove me to succeed. I had a burning desire to prove myself, and I don't think that's necessarily a bad thing. However, at the same time it caused me to seek perfection and external validation, and to measure my worth against others. The problem was: I was never perfect. I could never receive validation that was good enough to lift my self-worth. In turn I saw, everyone else as better than me. So even though I smiled, I was perpetually depressed, emotionally delicate, and easily knocked off my game.

Here's an example of an incident that illustrates perfectly my fragile state of being.

I wrote earlier about developing physical coping mechanisms as my vision deteriorated. One of the habits that naturally develops with a failing macula is called eccentric viewing; it's also called preferred retinal loci (PRL). It is a method by which the person looks slightly away from the subject in order to view it peripherally. In many cases of age-related macular degeneration, the individual may go on for years without noticing the failing vision. As the macula develops scotomas (scars that create blind spots) they naturally adjust their focus, moving the blind spots out of the way.

So over the years, I'd intuitively developed eccentric viewing techniques. But I was still pretending I didn't have a problem. I worked the sales floor by memory and believed nobody could tell I wasn't *"normal."* Then one day I was helping a customer explaining the difference between two brands of skis. Of course I'm looking at him sideways, because it's the only way I can see him. He mistakenly thought I wasn't giving him my full attention and snapped, "Hey, pal! I'm over here."

It was a punch to the solar plexus. I was humiliated. In my mind, he'd just said, *you are the biggest loser the world has ever seen. You think people don't know you're a defect? They do!*

I wanted to crawl in a hole and shovel dirt on my head. I guess in a way, I did: I went out and got very drunk that night.

Speaking of drunk, it would be appropriate to say I'd gained a certain reputation around town. It would also be fair to note that said reputation extended into the police department. I'd gotten into enough trouble, between the car crashes and over-the-top public intoxication, that my mug shot was most likely pinned on one of those corkboards they use for the FBI's most wanted lists. By this time I'd seen the front seat of plenty of police cars—yes, that's right, front seat. No matter how big the stunt, I always seem to avoid serious consequences. In today's world I know that wouldn't be the case. I slowly compiled a record that would have made me eligible for prison, and deservedly so. But back then I was still the little boy who'd been dealt a bad hand, and people felt sorry for me. I guess they could see that I wasn't malicious. I was hurting and always sincerely apologetic. I wanted to be normal, but I had zero staying power over alcohol. I'd manage to quit for a week or two, but one drink took me right back to where I'd left off.

I was growing increasingly frustrated with my life. My friends were away at school, preparing to live happily ever after. I'd fallen head over heels for Molly, and she was also away at college. And me? I was living at home with my parents, working an ordinary job with no promise of a future, and hanging out with the town derelicts. It was a very dark period that lasted about four years. It wasn't my darkest period by any means—that would come later—but nevertheless it was black. Once my eyes opened in the morning, I carried a singular focus throughout the day: I looked forward to party time, and everything in between was a necessary evil. I was determined to drink away the fear, drink away the inadequacies, and drown the haunting thoughts of failure. All the while I hungered for something more but I wasn't sure exactly what. I was stuck in a ditch with no idea how to get out.

Being stymied is something we've all experienced at one time or another. Having a heartfelt desire remain just out of reach, blocked by something we believe is out of our control. You are probably familiar with the feeling of tension that arises when that happens.

Frustration and its relationship to anger have been studied since 1939. Science has discovered frustration can produce feelings of anger, which in turn can generate feelings of aggression and then aggressive behavior. Someone may be frustrated with his job for whatever reason, but he can't scream at the boss and expect to remain employed. Therefore the person might redirect the frustration and anger toward his spouse or perhaps his children.

I was a living, breathing test case of the hypothesis. I was resentful that my life dreams had been stolen by some stupid vision disorder. I was mad that I had been cursed, been robbed. What frustrated me most, as you know, was not being able to drive. So what did I do when I got tipsy? I drove. And 99 percent of the time, it was at night: the worst possible time.

After a few drinks I'd steal a set of keys, anybody's keys, and then get behind the wheel and go fast. If you're adding up the variables—legally blind and drunk driving—and feeling a sense of disgust, I'm with you. It turns my stomach to think of how foolish I was. It is only by the grace of God that I am alive and never seriously hurt anyone. I've had to work long and hard to forgive myself, and after reading the whole story, I hope you will forgive me, too. How could I be so stupid? The answer is simple: I had a death wish. I wanted to die. And when someone's life has reached a point of utter despair, where the beauty of life has been distorted and twisted into something ugly, one doesn't make the best choices.

The back roads near my house were a speed demon's dream: long, rolling straightaways with an equal mix of soft and hairpin curves. That's where I would go to take out my frustrations and drive like a maniac. I remember ripping along one night, and I noticed a car pull close to my rear bumper. I assumed whoever it was wanted to race, so I punched the accelerator. I opened up a little distance, but not for long—he came flying up behind me again. When he got close enough, I slammed the brakes and heard his tires squeal, then sped off laughing, heading up a crest. I topped the hill going well over one hundred miles per hour and noticed flashing blue lights ahead in the distance. I figured the police must have pulled someone over. But then suddenly there was a set of lights on *my* tail, and I saw more closing in from the right. The next thing I knew, I had five police cars chasing after me. It turned out the first guy wasn't trying to race after all—he was a cop. But guess what? Nothing happened. No ticket, no arrest. All I got was, "Charlie, you've gotta stop this," as they drove me home.

As I've said earlier, there were never serious consequences for my behavior. I believe it was because people saw that there was potential. They were hopeful that one day I might turn the corner. So instead of tough love, which was what I needed, I had enablers; no one ever questioned my behavior. Every once in a while someone might look at me and say, "Look what you're doing to yourself." But I can't say that there was ever a sincere attempt at intervention.

There was a period of time where my older sister, Kathleen, and I crossed paths at my parents' house. She'd come back home with her infant daughter. Though she was disgusted with my parties and my less than a stellar group of friends, we fell into our old pattern. She had always been my protector, so when I'd go out and get plastered, she'd wait up until I made it home. She'd get me to bed when I couldn't make it on my own, and she did her best to hide me from our parents. Just like old times.

It was a similar situation at work. As one can imagine, heavy drinking coupled with lines of cocaine doesn't lend itself to punctuality and attendance. There were plenty of days where I couldn't get up because I'd just laid down. Or I'd show up to work looking like hell and smelling like a wino. When that happened at the ski shop, George covered for me.

I recall a time I took out the company van for a joy ride and made a pit stop at the 7-11 for more beer. I came out of the store swinging a twelve-pack, and a Cheshire cop was parked next to the van. He looked right at me and opened his door before I could duck and hide. As I said, I had a certain reputation around town. He knew exactly who I was; he knew that my eyes were shot and that I wasn't supposed to be driving.

"Who you with, Charlie?" he asked.

"I, um… I…" I was busted cold and couldn't even come up with a lie.

The general manager, the guy who managed six stores in our region, got the call. I figured he would fire me on the spot, and I'd be arrested. I was intoxicated behind the wheel without a driver's license. I'd become pretty adept at wiggling out of tough situations by then, but this time I was caught in the act.

Well, I didn't get fired. I didn't get arrested, and I didn't even get a ticket. What I got was a ride home. And get this: the next day at work, no one even mentioned the incident. Crazy, isn't it?

Even when someone did stand up, circumstances conspired to reward me for bad behavior. I once got fired and rehired at the same company in less than twenty-four hours, with a raise to boot.

I mentioned earlier during the summer months I worked for a company that built tennis courts, and I very quickly became foreman. It was the combination of my dad's work ethic, my need for validation, and my experience at Copper Valley. In other words, I knew what I was doing and was determined to outwork everybody in the company. I busted my tail during the day and partied hard at night. By this time, the disciples were home from college, and the five of us were living together in a house. I should mention I was the odd man out— that irresponsible roommate others wished would grow up. I didn't understand why anyone would refuse to down a beer because he had to get up early for work. I thought college had turned them into corporate stuffed shirts.

It just so happened that our company was building tennis courts in a development next to the house in which we lived. Being a foreman meant I had keys to everything. One night—or I should say early morning—I decided I wanted to drive a bulldozer, and that's what I did. I went next door, unlocked the gate, fired up the dozer, and went about moving dirt around. It wasn't long before I heard sirens, though. I hopped off and sprinted home before the cops arrived. When they came asking questions, of course I didn't know anything. I had no idea who might be silly enough to drive bulldozers at such a late hour, and I was appalled that someone would even be stupid enough to do such a thing. The cops knew it was me, but as usual they didn't press.

But they did notify the owner, and the next day he confronted me. "You have fun last night?" he asked, skipping all pleasantries when I walked into work. His eyes were like darts.

"What? What are you talking about?" I retorted with my standard response of having no knowledge of anything.

"Don't play dumb. You know what I'm—"

"What? I have no idea... what are you...?"

"You're fired!"

"For what?" I cried.

He turned and walked away.

I didn't give a crap. I didn't miss a beat. That afternoon I was out sealing driveways and feeling rather free.

The next day his son pulled up in the company van while I was finishing up a driveway. He said, "You're coming back to work tomorrow."

"But your dad fired me," I said, perplexed.

"We need you. Look, just be at work tomorrow morning. Okay?"

In a nanosecond it occurred to me I could probably get a raise. I said, "Yeah, I can come back—but I'll need a least a two-dollar-an-hour raise."

I got the raise and was back at work the next day.

Without consequences or anybody confronting me, I kept ratcheting up my recklessness until I did something that nearly killed me. To this day I don't understand why people stood still as I headed toward obvious destruction. The closest thing that came to confrontation was a letter from one of the disciples; he wrote it after I misbehaved at a wedding reception. Alcohol was involved—too much alcohol, I should say. In the letter he told me how disappointed he was. He could no longer look up to me like he did when we were growing up. He said I was throwing my life away, and it was a shame.

I was outraged! How dare he say that about me! He had no idea what it was like to be me; he didn't understand my pain. I was blind and he wasn't. All he needed to do was spend one second in my shoes, and he'd know. He'd know how much pain I was in and why I had to drink. I tore the letter to shreds and grabbed a beer.

CHAPTER 13

Imagine my life as an acoustic guitar. Then imagine each negative thought, every negative action, torqueing the peg heads just a little tighter. At a minimum, one day the strings are going to pop. However, there's a chance something even more catastrophic could happen. It's possible for stress to compromise the structural integrity of the neck, and one day it'd cave in. I believe something similar to this was what happened to me. The accumulating stress, a single thought at a time, eventually concluded in a cataclysmic event after returning home from a Grateful Dead concert in New York City.

Initially, my brother was supposed to go with his friends Pete and Sean. I only inherited the ticket when he decided to be responsible and not go out on a work night. I had no such instinct and jumped at a chance to see the Dead no matter where or when they were performing. And this show was in New York City—the Big Apple! Madison Square Garden! There was no way I could turn down a chance to meet a bunch of friends I hadn't met yet. These people were as interested as I was to ingest substances and get rightly tuned for the psychedelic ride with the maestro, Jerry Garcia.

I was pumped and had been anticipating the show for days. My buddy, who was a wicked Deadhead, even gave me his sweater to wear. It was perfect with shades of red and purple and blue that melted into each other in a trippy swirl. It was a Dead sweater if I'd ever seen one.

I started to party early that day; by three o'clock I'd already had a couple of beers. When they came to get me, I was well along the way to feeling pretty good. We smoked some pot, picked up a couple more six-packs, and headed for the New Haven train station to hop on the Metro North. We snuck the beers onboard and started knocking them back as soon as the coast was clear. I remember that as we approached Grand Central Station, the train filled with more Deadheads: jeans, tie-dye, dreadlocks, and the smells of good marijuana, patchouli, and sage. It was good vibes the whole way.

After we got off the train, we headed for one of the corner liquor stores that made New York a drunk's dream; we grabbed more tall boys. Then we tripped around with all the Tour Rats outside the show. My typical pre-show methodology was to take a hit of this, a toke of that, and maybe drop a couple of tabs. But that night all I did was drink. Well, I did buy a couple of balloons and remember being knocked to my knees from whippet (nitrous oxide) hits.

The concert was amazing, classic Jerry. He took all thirty-nine thousand of us on one giant roller-coaster ride.

Afterward, though obviously buzzed, I'd insisted that we get more beer for the ride home. I mean, who wanted to ride two hours without a beer in hand? Certainly not me. We hit one of those drunk's dreams and grabbed a couple more sixers. The start of the train ride home was uneventful and seemed it would be like any other. But remember, I was drunk and was still drinking. I was pouring it on and reaching the point where the anger surfaced. That night the face of anger was more excitement, more booze, and more recklessness.

After about a half hour, I was at the point where I'd look for a set of keys or go next door and hop on a bulldozer, but I was stuck on the train. I began to wander through the cars, beer in hand, looking for something to get into. I'd been known to punch out windows. I'd even started trouble with people twice my size. I was the obnoxious drunk, tipsy to my eyeballs and wandering the cars of Metro North.

I was in between cars, in that middle space that's ensconced by the accordion-like rubber, when I heard and felt the wind, and I stopped dead in my tracks. I looked to my right and noticed there was a sliver of space in the rubber. As the train undulated, the opening moved like fish gills. I walked over, looked at it for a second, and then stuck my hand out. The rush of damp night air against my hand instantly gave a promise of the sensation I'd craved from as long as I could remember. That feeling I first noticed out on the boat with my dad: speed.

I pressed my torso between the rubber and stuck my face in the wind. It was better than pure bliss. The feel of forty-five-mile-per-hour wind flattening the flesh on my face, whipping my hair into a frenzy, and taking my breath away. I stayed there for I don't know how long, bathing in the sensation with my eyes closed.

When I opened my eyes I noticed there was a ladder, and that's when I got one of my ideas. I thought, *how cool it would be to sit on top of the train and drink beer? That would be the ultimate.* I'd pulled a bunch of insane stunts up till then, but nothing like that. This one would make me a legend back home; I could hear them telling me how crazy I was. The ladder was right there—easy as pie. So what the hell? I decided to go for it.

Naturally, I had to go find Pete and Sean because they needed to at least see me do it. But if I had my way, they'd come up with me. I hustled through the train and finally found them. I said, "You guys gotta come and see what I found. It's sick!"

I lead them back to the opening and climbed through, as if I'd done it a hundred times. This time I pulled my entire body through the accordion with my beer still in hand. I was in heaven. The train was full speed ahead, and the sound alone lit a fire in me. It was a deep metal, muscular, swooshing and click-clacking over the tracks. I was flying high.

The danger was obvious: one false step and it was over. But it was better than any drug I could imagine. My endorphins were raging, adrenaline was at maximum dosage, and my heart was a ten-thousand-pound gorilla rattling my ribs. I started up the ladder, but when I looked behind me, Sean and Pete weren't there anymore, so I climbed down to sell them on the idea. "Guys, come on. It'll be so cool. You gotta do this with me. Come on!"

It would take two more tries, but eventually I convinced them to follow me. I chalk it up to being a good salesman. I'd been persuading people out of their comfort zones for years—which, I understand, had always been my gift.

In your mind's eye, look down on the train as it sped along in darkness, and I'll tell you what happened next.

I'd reached the top of the car, Sean was nearing the top rung, and Pete was beginning the climb. I found a spot and sipped my beer just as Sean poked his head over the edge, still holding on to the ladder; I remember him surveying the top of the car. Then he pointed at something behind me and said, "Whatever you do, don't touch that."

I'd missed whatever it was and turned to see what he was referring too… And even with my crappy eyes, I could read the bold white letters that said, "Danger: Extreme High Voltage."

That was just about the time the train rocked, and my life changed forever.

The unexpected movement caused me to lose my balance. My natural instinct was to grab hold of something to keep from falling. What I clutched was twelve thousand volts of red-hot Metro North electricity. The juice ricocheted through my body and shot out my ankles with such force that it almost knocked Sean off the ladder. He ended up blind for two days in the hospital with flash burns on his face. Even Pete suffered minor burns, though he hadn't even made it past the bottom rung.

CHAPTER 14

I brought the Metro North to a dead stop. Ten cars and a hundred-plus tons of charging steel, glass, and high-impact plastics limped, fizzled, and died.

But, I was still alive. Yes, I was alive.

Thus far I've only talked about my psychological suffering and nothing of the physical pain that went along with the fear-driven recklessness. I was always in the emergency room for something or another: bloody lacerations, broken bones from falling off my skateboard or headfirst out of a tree; tumbling end over end on my motocross bike and skidding shirtless and without a helmet across hot summer asphalt. My skill set with the written word is not adequate to describe the torture I put my body through. However, every broken bone, scrape, and contusion combined, then multiplied by ten, couldn't equal the realm I had just entered. Looking back, I realize that severe road rash over 80 percent of my body was baby stuff.

I was alive and quickly put a couple of thoughts together. First, I realized this was not like any of my other mishaps—and I was scared. I was in unthinkable pain and could smell *my* flesh burning. My second thought was, *I need to get off the top of the car.* I then went into a state that you'll recognize if you've ever been in a life-or-death situation. There's a powerful survival instinct that lies dormant in all of us: think of the husband who somehow lifts a burning car off his wife's legs.

I gathered my wits and by some means managed my way down the ladder. When I got to the bottom, I fell, tumbled, and rolled, ending up underneath the train writhing in pain. I screamed into the night,

"My arm! My arm! My arm! Something's wrong with my arm!" But nobody could hear me. In fact, Metro personnel were trying to figure out cause of the malfunction so that they could keep their schedule. Had it not been for Sean hollering to get help, they may have restarted and run me over.

High-voltage electricity can do a serious number on the body. On one end of the spectrum, there's death. The juice can sizzle you to a brittle crisp—literally burn you to death. A notch down the damage spectrum, the surge can stop a heart or shut down the lungs and other vital organs. It can cause quadriceps muscles to contract with enough force to snap a femur in half. Along the pathway where it enters and exits, vital organs are affected by the flow of energy, the heat. Simply stated, it can cook your insides; that's why I smelled flesh burning. All that was bad enough. What ended up being my biggest issue, however, was the exit wounds. I had eight of them in varying degrees of severity. I was screaming about my right arm because it had won the award for most mangled.

The juice entered my body and had to get out. And boy oh boy, did it make a dramatic exit. It blew a cantaloupe-sized hole in my left side just below my rib cage. It shot out both ankles—that's what hit Sean in the face—the back of both knees, under both armpits, and my arm. When I say it "blew holes" in my body, that isn't metaphor or hyperbole; that's literally what happened. The electricity exploded out of my body, leaving fleshy-raw, puckered, asymmetrical wounds that defied cosmetic repair. My arm was such a mess that they wanted to amputate.

While lying under the train, I began to fade in and out of consciousness. As a result I remember the night much like time-lapsed scenes in a movie montage; they meld together, fading in a dreamlike sequence that's not necessarily linear. Before I move on, I should note how alone I felt. I don't remember seeing Sean or Pete or anyone else for that matter; it was just me. It was as if I was the only person in the world, and the thought of dying that way hit me hard.

According to Sean, the ambulance took at least forty minutes to arrive. It was just my luck: I'd stalled the train in an area that wasn't readily accessible, so they had to wobble slowly over the tracks. In the meantime the pain was otherworldly; every second was an eternity. Eventually there reached a point where I couldn't take it anymore and passed out. The next thing I knew, I woke up in the ambulance.

I remember the soothing sensation of cool water being poured on my chest, and I looked into the face of the paramedic. He was seated next to me with three rows of gallon water jugs lined up on the floor. He'd cap one, start at my head, and slowly move the length of my body, ending at my feet. Oh my God, did that water feel good! It gave me temporary relief from the burning. By the time he was at my feet I was begging him, "Please do it again."

He poured a few more gallons before he took out a pair of scissors and set aim on the wicked Dead sweater. "Hey!" I said. "You can't cut the sweater—it's not mine. My friend will be pissed at me."

He smiled. "I don't think your friend will mind." He cut a straight line from my navel to my chest.

The last thing I remember was asking who in the hell was doing the driving. It felt like they were purposely hitting every pothole in the city. Every time the stretcher rattled, it caused immense pain.

CHAPTER 15

I woke up in what I'd describe as unfolding layers of awareness, in stages. I lingered in one space like a child learning to walk, catching my balance before taking the next step. A maximum dose of morphine had something to do with the world opening up the way it did.

The first thing I took in was bright white walls and fluorescent lights overhead. I wasn't quite sure where I was until the smell registered. I'd spent enough time in hospitals, emergency rooms, and such, and the scent was etched in my nostrils. A mixture of rubbing alcohol and early stages of human decay, like death. Hospitals had always smelled like death to me.

It was then that I remembered the accident and started checking for damage.

I saw that I was wrapped in gauze from head to toe. Yards and yards of sterile white cotton wound all over my body. The only things that weren't wrapped were my eyes, and they appeared to be just as crappy as ever. While surveying the gauze, I noticed a freeway of intersecting tubes and wires coming from somewhere on my body. Then I became aware of machines beeping and hissing softly in the background, their cadence like human breath. Suddenly a priest came into view, and he was praying.

I'm dead. I thought. *I must have died, and this must be some kind of weird... Wait, hold on... Wait a second!*

I'd been an altar boy, so even in my morphine-induced stupor, it came to me what was going on: the priest was anointing me, delivering my last rites. He was preparing me for a journey on to wherever he thought I was going.

I was instantly angry. I'd been pissed at God for as long as I could remember. I was ticked at him for making me defective; he didn't *have* to make me loser, but he did. If it was absolutely necessary to infect four of the Collins children, he could have easily swapped my eyes with one of my sisters'. They'd both said many times that if they could, they would trade with me. So all the stories about God and his infinite love was a pile of horse crap, as far as I was concerned. God didn't love me. Not Charlie Collins.

Right then, I decided I was going to live. If God and his agent thought I was going to die, I'd show them. I was just about to give the priest a piece of my mind when my mother appeared. She was just in time for me to tell her, "Get him out of here! I'm not going to die!"

And obviously I didn't. I've got to tell you, though, there were times during the rehab when the pain was so excruciating that I wished I'd had. It was major league hurt, well beyond anything I'd ever felt. It was so bad that it forced me to enter a new dimension. Mentally I went into this place that I can't readily explain. I had to, though—because there was pain, and then there was something else. What I dealt with was something else altogether. Think of that beating Rambo took in *First Blood*. Remember him morphing into that blank gaze—the red glow of fire in his eyes while the camera slowly zoomed in? I had to find that place or else the pain would have destroyed me. I always loved a good challenge, so I turned the pain into a test... It was an examination, however, that I came close to never taking. When I learned the plan for my arm, I tried to kill myself right there in the hospital.

They wanted to cut it off at the elbow; I'm guessing because I touched the voltage with my right hand, that arm had the worst of the exit wounds. I mentioned that electricity doesn't enter and then gently exit your body; it leaves a trail of destruction and crescendos with a bang, blowing flesh inside out. Well, think of the anatomy of a forearm—the intricate design of muscles, arteries, veins, and tendons working in unison to simply move your fingers. Much of that was destroyed. After the incident the inside of my forearm from the elbow to almost my wrist was mutilated, raw flesh. But twenty-four hours later it was swollen like one of Popeye's forearms, festering, immobile, and dying on the vine.

The first doctor that looked at it did his best to keep a poker face, but I read his slight frown. He was thinking, *I can't fix this. I'm gonna have to cut it off.* He held my arm up, calculating. *Right there, at the elbow.* He gave me this grave look and said apologetically, "I'm afraid you're going to lose your arm. I'll try to save as much of it as possible."

I thought, *This guy must be crazy.* "There's no way in hell I'm letting you do that!" I said.

"But you'll never have use of the arm—"

"You're not cutting off my arm!" I screamed.

My parents were in the room at the time, and I looked at them both, pleading. "You can't let them cut off my arm. There's no way… Just kill me. I will not go through this life with one arm and bad eyesight."

"I'm afraid there's no other way," the doctor said, and he left the room.

When night fell, I was alone with the thought of a life with one arm in addition to legal blindness, and it was more than I could take. God had already screwed me in the eye department, and now he wanted my arm? It was time to die.

I was still in intensive care and connected to a collection of machines. Blood and oxygen and antibiotics, pain medicine and vital fluids, all being delivered by a central venous catheter sunk in the center of my chest. The wires and tubes bloomed from that central point, crisscrossed, and ran into the bank of equipment behind my bed. I gathered up enough strength to grab a fist-full of wires and yanked. Tubes came loose, spilling fluids on the floor; equipment toppled and bells started ringing like a six-alarm fire. Nurses rushed in my room in a frenzy and worked quickly to get me reconnected. Eventually the doctor showed up and sat at my beside. He looked at me and softly asked, "Why? Why, did you do that, Charlie?"

"I will not live without my arm," I said. "If you can't find someone to fix it, just turn off the machines. I'd rather die than live with one arm."

The next day I met with a specialist. He examined my arm and reiterated what the first doctor had said. He didn't think my arm was salvageable, but he said he would try. "There is no guarantee," he said. "In fact, you should be prepared for the worst."

I told him, "If you do your part, I'll do mine, and my arm will be okay. I already know it."

Those words turned out to be a glimpse into my future. I'd created the reality I wanted, and all my actions from that point forward fell in line with the idea of first saving my arm and second, walking out of the hospital whole. That's all I wanted, and I would do anything to achieve the result. It allowed me to deal with the pain because I knew what was waiting for me on the other side.

I ended up having a number of surgeries on my arm, the majority being skin grafts. However, the very first procedure was a fasciotomy. Fascia surrounds the muscles, providing a supportive and movable wrapping for nerves and blood vessels as they pass through and between the muscles. With my arm swelling and steadily pressing against the fascia, it would eventually kill those same nerves and blood vessels. In layman's terms, my arm would wither and die while still attached to my body. The doctor cut the fascia to release the pressure, and guess what? It worked! I could move my fingers right after the surgery.

Next began the process of debridement (removing the dead skin) and keeping my wounds clean. I should add before I move forward that in addition to the open exit wounds on my ankles, knees, armpits, torso, and forearm—protocol requires the doctor to leave the incisions open—I had second-degree flash burns on my face. It looked like I'd sat in the July sun for three days straight, lathering my mug in baby oil.

I entered this phase of my rehab in good spirits. In addition to the successful surgery on my arm, the other good news was there seemed to be nothing wrong with my internal organs. However, I was by no means out of the woods. With a compromised immune system, the doctors were concerned about the possibility of sepsis, a severe systemic infection in which bacteria enters the blood stream.

Everyday a female nurse would come to my room and strip me down to my birthday suit. I remember a feeling of utter vulnerability that came with her visits; I was completely helpless and all I could do was try to cover myself. Metaphorically I was a newborn—I couldn't walk because of the wounds on my ankles and knees, and I only had use of one arm. But I needed her help if I was going to get better, so I surrendered.

She wheeled me into a room where they put me in a harness and slowly lowered me into a giant vat of bubbling saline solution for fifteen minutes. If you just winced, you should have; the thought still causes me to shudder. The salt baths served a dual purpose of keeping the wounds clean and loosening the dead skin. The first day I screamed at the top of my lungs because it hurt so badly. I was on maximum doses of morphine, and still it was more than I thought I could stand.

After the salt baths, I would spend time scraping away dead skin from my face with a straight razor. I thought the salt baths were painful until I started that process. It was severe, acute, unbearable, raging, racking, splitting—pick your own word for pain and insert here; now multiply by one hundred. However, by day three I figured it was as bad as it would get. It was then I crossed over into that Rambo dimension. I psyched up mentally when it was treatment time and met the pain head-on. I was following my intuition, allowing it to guide me toward healing. And a funny thing happened along the way: I met my true calling for the first time.

There was a ten-year-old who arrived in my ward with third-degree burns on his face and hands. He'd discovered some of his father's bullets in the basement, taken them apart, and dumped the gunpowder in a pile. Then he thought to stick a match on the pile and see what would happen. The gunpowder exploded in his face. By the time he showed up, I had taken to popping one-handed wheelies up and down the halls in my wheelchair. One day I ended up in his room. I still get goose bumps when I envision him lying there in tears. It lit something inside me that I didn't realize was there: empathy.

You've learned enough about my life to understand the magic of that moment. My whole life had been about fear and pain and "poor Charlie." But when I saw that kid, frightened and uncertain of the future, I had this overwhelming urge to help him. For the first time that I could recall, it wasn't about me. I began to visit his room daily. I'd power through my naked salt baths and razor scraping, and then I'd hurry to his room. We'd watch movies, laugh, and hang out. I had a remote control car that we raced up and down the halls, terrorizing the floor. Through the process I managed to convince him that everything was going to be fine, and lo and behold, he got better!

Looking back, I count that as the first time I used my power of persuasion for something good. I wasn't doing it because I wanted him to like me. I wasn't doing it because I wanted something in return. It was selfless; I did it because I saw he was afraid and needed a guide. I still have the plaque his parents sent me as thanks for helping their son heal.

There was another kid, a nineteen-year-old that arrived after an accident in a convertible Cutlass. The car flipped, and he slid fifty yards over the asphalt, leaving most of his skin on the pavement. There were times when I could hear him wailing from rooms away. I would wheel my chair down to his room and sit with him. And get this: my words to him were, "You're not gonna make it if you don't have the right attitude." That's right—Mr. Bad Attitude himself was lecturing someone else on the virtues of attitude. At the time I had no idea what I was doing. I was inspired and moving in spirit. I somehow got the key to unlock a spiritual principal that was lying dormant. I gave of myself without expectations. It was pure love, pure service. By doing so I got well faster than anyone could understand.

The initial estimates about the length of my stay, based upon patients with similar burns was three months. I went home in three weeks. Another miracle, they said.

CHAPTER 16

You're probably thinking, "Okay, he almost killed himself, then went through hellish pain recovering, and on top of it all, he found his calling. That had to have been like Saul of Tarsus transforming into Paul the Apostle, after meeting Jesus on the road to Damascus—an incident so profound that it could only change a person for the better." That's what you're thinking, right?

Well, yes, I did change. But not in the way you might think.

I went back to my parents' house to finish my recovery and was as pious as my nickname Padre might indicate. I didn't drink, didn't smoke any pot, and didn't do lines of coke. I'd bought in to the hype that I was a miracle. I had purpose—I had no idea what it was, but I knew it couldn't be drinking and doing drugs. I'd survived something that should have killed me. I was alive for a reason, and I needed to figure it out. I locked into my iron will and did what former First Lady Nancy Reagan so naively suggested: I just said no. Boy, was that a bad move.

Trying to use willpower against addiction is like expecting a colony of ants to stop a herd of stampeding elephants. I didn't have a shot. And for those of you who think Mrs. Reagan was on to something, I'll paraphrase what the research experts say: willpower is not a reliable tool when striving for change.[4] But of course you know that already. I'm sure

---

[4]   Jonah Lehrer, *Blame It on the Brian: The Wall Street Journal*, (December 26, 2009) http://online.wsj.com/news/articles/SB1000142405274870347870457461 12052322122442

you've made one of those grand New Year's Day resolutions only to see it crumble well before Valentine's Day.

First off, we underestimate the extent to which we're influenced by our surroundings; we are truly creatures of habit. So if one wants change, one place to start is with the physical environment or routine. Of course I didn't have a clue and went right back into the conditions where my addiction began. I saw the same friends and fell back into the same routine. Triggers lurked around every corner. But I fought, locked in, and stayed sober. I was a miracle, and soon the nagging in my gut about my life's purpose would be answered. It never occurred to me that I was on earth to help, to give of myself unselfishly. Even though I had experienced the blessings of giving without expectations, it wouldn't sink in until much later that I was to live that experience as my vocation.

It's amazing that I was able stay clean for the sixty days that I did. And let me tell you, when I took that first drink, the floodgates opened—my addiction roared back with the vengeance. I was instantly back to my old ways, as if I'd never left. But thanks to the train accident, I was new and improved. Remember the grit I'd developed sitting in the salt baths? The pain I told you about scraping dead skin off my face with a razor? It had made me numb, so to speak. The fear and questioning why I was alive without an answer turned my world to muted shades of gray. I couldn't find joy in anything. There was a constant ache in the center of my soul coupled with a sense of impending doom. The miracle of surviving the accident slowly shifted into what I believed was the precursor of violent death. And because I'd actually made an attempt at suicide, I didn't have any fear; on the contrary, I feared living more than death. Living was twice the pain of the salt baths, and I'd never found the frame of mind to successfully deal with it. *It would be easier just to die*, I thought. I knew it wouldn't be much longer before I lost all hope. Then I would kill myself for sure—drive my motorcycle in the path of an eighteen-wheeler. I was just going through the motions, waiting for the day.

In the meantime, my external projection was all smiles: good ol' good-timing Charlie. I wore the Metro North scars as a badge of honor. Everywhere I went, people knew me as the crazy guy who got electrocuted by the train and lived. I basked in the attention for as long as I could, but eventually the story went stale. There is a finite number of times any story can be told After a while, I realized I had nowhere to go; there was nothing else I could offer the world.

My mother was on the verge of a nervous breakdown while watching my free-fall. My parents prayed the accident would serve as a wake-up call. When it became clear that it had in fact drove me deeper into the abyss, they feared for my life. It was obvious I was marching toward catastrophe. I was drinking and doing drugs at a pace that was impossible for it to end well. My mother was certain my end would come when I decided to make a return trip to Madison Square Garden, almost one year to the day of my accident, to see the Dead of course. She begged me not to go, fearing I would never make it home. He fear was well founded because I almost didn't.

I took the train with a group of about fourteen friends, and as custom dictated, we got fully intoxicated along the way. This time, while outside the concert mingling with the Tour Rats, I took a little of whatever I could get my hands on: acid, mushrooms, weed, whatever ended up in my hand got ingested. By the time the concert started, I was high out of my mind. I remember bits and pieces from the start of the show, but that's about it. From there, a six-hour block of time is unaccounted for, and I have no idea what happened. The next thing I remember is waking—not from sleep but rather from whatever combination of drugs I'd taken—in a room full of about twenty-five strangers who were as high or higher than I was. I had no clue where I was or how I had got there. When I started asking questions and tried to get to the bottom of the situation, all I got were blank stares and, "I don't know, dude."

I bailed and began wandering the streets of New York at 3:30 in the morning, looking for Grand Central Station. To this day I don't know where I was, and I count myself lucky to have made it home. The streets of New York could have turned into a bad place for a lost, blind man.

I eventually I found my way to Penn Station and jumped on the train. I was out of money, and when the conductor came to ask for my ticket, I pleaded with him not to kick me off. He was compassionate and allowed me to stay, thank goodness. I arrived at the New Haven station and placed a call home. I don't think the phone even rang; my mother picked it up so quickly. She screamed, "Oh, thank God, you're alive! You're going to worry me to death, Charlie. I was worried sick. Where were you?"

I'm sure you're wondering how I got separated from my friends. Well, apparently I stormed off in a huff when someone in our group told me to take it easy during the show. Remember, I was at the lowest point of my life; my default emotion when under the influence was anger. The face of anger I wore that night was an obnoxious, belligerent jackass, and of course, no one had the right to call me on it. No one understood my pain or had lived in my shoes. I was the one who was blind, and I had a right to feel the way I did. So as I'd been known to do when confronted, I bailed. My friends told me they waited until the last train. When I didn't show, they assumed I'd gone home.

It wasn't too long after the concert when I decided life *was* worth living, and I felt it was time to put a stop to the pain. I was working a meaningless, dead-end, landscaping job and did not find joy in anything I did. I couldn't drink the pain away, and I couldn't snort enough cocaine to quiet the voices. It was clear I wasn't fit to be alive. As I lay in my bed night after night, the emotional pain seemed to incrementally increase until it drove me into a corner. I was going to do something in the next couple of days.

It may have been the very next day that I was cutting the grass at Willows Motorsports, the local motorcycle dealership. I'd go there once a week and drive the lawnmower for a credit account in the parts department. I used the account to keep the motocross bike I'd purchased off the showroom floor in tip-top order. When I needed a release, I would rip through the woods behind my parents' house like a madman. By that time, I'd been a Willows customer for years, and my unbridled joy for bikes was well-known. I imagine I was their most enthusiastic customer by a long shot; I knew the entire staff and could talk shop with anyone in the building.

On this particular day, I'd finished my job and was walking the sales floor to stare at the lineup. For me, looking at a bike is equal to what Playboy is for most men. I was lost in fantasy, in visions of riding top-end and taking jumps, when I felt a tap on my shoulder. I turned around and looked into the face of the owner, Jimbo.

Jimbo was this big, burly dude with a long, silvery beard who looked like he belonged in ZZ Top. I'd been going to Willow's for years, and Jimbo was the closest thing to a God that I knew. He was this cool-looking dude who owned a motorcycle dealership. Plus, he had a reputation as a badass. That being said, is there any wonder I almost wet myself when he said, "Hey, Charlie, I was wondering if you would like to work here?"

CHAPTER 17

Have you ever been hit with something so unexpected that it renders you speechless? Your limbs freeze while your brain uses all available energy for a massive computation. Coherent speech is impossible because what words you can manage crash into a pile at the tip of your tongue. That's what happened to me when Jimbo asked me to work there. I imagine he thought I was spastic, staring at him with an opened-mouthed, blank gaze.

He'd caught me off guard. I was completely taken by surprise when I turned and saw it was him. Of course my knee-jerk thought was, *He's firing me.* Although I kept the grass as perfect as the outfield at Fenway Park, he'd surely found that one blade of grass I'd missed. I expected, and almost always got, the short end of the stick. So when he asked if I wanted to work for him, my database crashed. Why would Jimbo ask *me*, of all people? I was a loser, a misfit who wasn't very smart. I'm sure he knew my reputation—everyone did. It had to be some kind of cruel trick. All this raced through my mind.

I managed to get out, "Um, what were you thinking?"

"Sales," Jimbo said. "Look, you're in here all the time. You know as much about this stuff as anybody. I think you'd be good at it."

By then my heart was beating so quickly that I thought I might faint. "Let me get back to you on that," I said. I turned, wanting badly to run, but I kept my composure and hurried out of the building.

I arrived home in a state of complete confusion. For the life of me, I couldn't get my mind around what he was thinking. Why did he ask *me*? Perhaps if I hadn't bailed out of there so quickly, I would have thought to ask. But as it was, I was scared out of my mind. I liked Jimbo, and the thought of being around motorcycles was beyond a dream, but there was no way I could take that job. I wasn't smart enough—everyone knew that, especially my friends. If I went to work for Jimbo, he'd find it out, too, and then he wouldn't like me. There was no way I could say yes.

I needed to talk to someone, so I went into the kitchen where my mom was making dinner. "Guess what?" I said as I took a seat at the table.

My tone caused immediate alarm. She stopped what she was doing and warily took a chair on the other side of the table, bracing for the latest edition of bad news. No words—she simply sat there waiting for the blow.

I blurted, "Jimbo asked if I wanted to work for him."

There was a slight delay before her eyes shot wide with excitement. It had been such a long time since anything good had come my way, and she was caught off guard, too. "Jimbo at Willows?" she asked. I nodded yes. "That's great, Charlie!" she cried. "You love motorcycles. I'm so happy for you!"

She breathed a sigh of relief and waited for me to give her the details, but all I did was sit quietly staring down at the tablecloth.

"What would you be doing?" she asked, sensing my trepidation.

"Sales."

"That's perfect for you. You know so much about—"

"What do you think I should do?" I looked up at her for an answer.

Her brow furrowed in confusion. "What do you mean?"

"Do you think I should take the job? Should I? I mean, I don't know if I can do it."

"Stop!" she demanded. "What's to think about? You love motorcycles. You know everything about them. You'll do great, Charlie."

Her encouragement was being drowned out by the voices in my head. *You're blind, Charlie. You'll never amount to anything. Don't waste Jimbo's time. Just say no and move on.*

She noticed the wheels churning and grabbed my hands. I'll never forget the sincerity in her voice while her eyes pleaded with me. She wanted so badly for me to see in myself what she'd seen for years. "You're smart, Charlie." She spoke in that soothing tone reserved for mothers. "And you work hard. Jimbo would be lucky to have you. What, do you think he'd ask just anybody to work for him?"

I didn't buy into the idea that I might be smart, because mothers are supposed to say that stuff. However, she'd said something that struck a chord. *Do you think he'd ask just anybody to work for him?*

I chewed on that thought the rest of day. I'm thinking, Jimbo *was* successful. He really wouldn't ask just anybody to work for him. In knowing that, I'd found a kernel of hope. I decided that Jimbo was smart—that much was obvious—and if he'd asked me to work for him, he must see something. I actually went to bed sober that night; it had been a long, long time since I'd done that. I lay there struggling with what I now realize equated to life or death: take the job or pass. I believe that had I turned down the opportunity, I would have been dead before the month was up.

At some point I decided to pray. I was skeptical, but my back was against the wall, and I didn't know what else to do. I told the same God that hated me, who had created me as a misfit, blind, drunk loser still living at home, "I need some help here."

I went on to tell him how I couldn't go on much longer. If he was real, he needed to show up and tell me what to do. "I'm lost and need a sign. Please, help me." I dozed off into the most restful night of sleep I'd had in a long time.

I woke the next morning refreshed and knowing I should take the job. I was sure it was the right thing to do. I also woke with a new outlook on my eye disorder. It was time for me to embrace who I was. *I am legally blind,* I thought. *There is no cure. There is nothing that's going to change. I'm going to tell Jimbo everything.*

Now that was a scary thought. It lit that incessant voice of fear inside my head. *Don't tell him! Once you tell him, you're done. He's never going to let a handicap sell motorcycles in his store. He'll think you're a loser.* But I had to do it. Even if it meant exposing all the dreams I'd just allowed myself to have: a life of motorcycles, snowmobiles, and ATVs could poof and vanish before they even got started.

When I got to the dealership, I went in his office and sat down. I was a bundle of nerves, my heart raced like my first date with Molly.

"So, what's the verdict?" he asked.

"I would love to take the job," I said. "But I need you to know I'm legally blind. I have an eye disorder called macular degeneration that affects my central vision. And if I work here, I'll need special equipment to do the job." My eyes fell into my lap as I steeled for the letdown.

He said very nonchalantly, "That's fine. What do we need to do?"

My life changed in an instant. Suddenly the world was Kawasaki green and Yamaha blue! The ache in my chest was swept away in a tidal wave of hope and excitement. I sat up straight and pushed my shoulders back. I said, "I'll call the state, and they'll get me everything I need. I don't need a lot, just something to help me read—a magnifier and some special computer software."

"Sounds good," he said. "Get what you need and let me know how I can help."

"Okay, I will."

"You'll start on a ninety-day probation, and after that we'll see what happens."

I was flabbergasted. I'd just told him I was defective, and it didn't matter. He still wanted me to work for him! I don't think my feet touched the ground the rest of the day. I finally felt good about just being Charlie.

Jimbo came into my life in the nick of time. He literally saved my life. Not with words but with his actions, he told me I wasn't a loser or a misfit. And I heard him. I belonged, I had something to offer, and I wasn't just using up valuable oxygen. Maybe I was smart. He opened up a whole new world of possibilities. He gave me hope, and the voices suddenly changed their negative dialogue. My thoughts went from dwelling in what I couldn't do to thinking only of what I *could* do. Amazingly, the desire to drink and do drugs vanished. I'd found a new drug. I had been born anew. I was brimming with energy and charged into the work like I did everything else, full throttle.

I called my state counselor and got set up with a CCTV (a reading machine) so that I could magnify print and read anything and everything ever printed in the history of the universe about motorcycles. I devoured information day and night. I got computer software for text-to-speech, as well as a pocket magnifier so I could spot-read on the sales floor. My intentions were to use it no matter who was looking. I wasn't ashamed anymore.

I asked Jimbo if I could make some changes and started by painting the interior bright green and blue. I wasn't a great painter, but I was motivated. I hung large print signs on every piece of equipment: sales pricing, monthly financing options. I did it for me, so that at a glance I could quote numbers, but it turned out to be something the customers loved. I set my reading machine up in the back office; its footprint was just a little larger than a computer. I installed the computer software. And presto, I was ready to rock and roll.

To the novice eye, nothing looked different—which reinforces my earlier assertion that hiring a person with visual impairment is a win-win. The equipment is nonintrusive, and I can just about guarantee you'll be hiring someone as eager as I was to make good.

I brought genuine, heartfelt zest and intuitive marketing ideas to Willows Motorsport, and sales began to climb. I did so well that three years later I was appointed vice president.

It was an ironic turn of events that Vegas's best odds makers could not have thought a possibility. Here I was, the guy who gave up on his brain in the eighth grade. As you know, I'd only stepped foot on college campuses for purposes of entertainment. Yet I was the first of my friends to really make it. I was running a multimillion-dollar sales department while they were still trying to gain traction with their degrees. It was a three-year fairy tale, a slow climb to the peak of the world's highest roller coaster. But like they say, what goes up must come down.

CHAPTER 18

I began my career at Willows in 1991. Over the course of next three years, my life bloomed into something so extraordinarily beautiful that it didn't seem real. If it were a movie script, the producer's notes would read, "You gotta rewrite this. It's too perfect—nobody will buy it." Professionally and personally, everything was clicking on all cylinders.

My relationship with Molly, after years of encouragement to dump her boyfriend, had officially began her junior year of college. We saw each other every weekend while she was away at school. I would take the two-hour train to Rhode Island to visit her most of the time, and occasionally she would drive home. By the time I got hired at Willows, it was clear there was no other woman I would ever love. I asked her to marry me on Valentine's Day 1992. Now, keep in mind that we'd known each other since grammar school, and we'd even worked together at the ski shop. She knew all about me—my dirty, filthy laundry—and still she said yes. There are lots of things I screwed up, but when I picked my wife, I hit a grand slam. I believe when all is said and done, there will be an application submitted on her behalf for sainthood, and I'm sure it will be rubber stamped by the committee. Though I gave her more than enough reasons to throw in the towel, she didn't do it. She will tell you, "I married Charlie for better or worse. I'm not going to run just because it gets hard."

In the professional arena, I experienced success that was well beyond anything Jimbo could have expected. He had a hunch that I was a natural sales talent with great instincts about bikes, and my enthusiasm was obvious. When that mixture combined with my burning desire to achieve and to show the world that I was good, that I was smart, business thrived. I thrived. All of that maniacal energy I had been using to destroy myself was pointed at work.

I've always had a need to understand how things work; it's in my nature to take things apart so that I might figure out how the components complement each other. I figure a tweak here, a tweak there, and I can make anything perform better. That mindset came into play wherever I worked. I would silently dream of being the owner and played with ideas of how I could make the business perform optimally. With Jimbo's blessing, that's what I did at Willows. First I devoured everything I could about the business of selling motorcycles, watercraft, and snowmobiles: financing, sales, marketing, and promotions. If it had anything to do with selling our merchandise, I read about it. I studied upcoming product improvements, sales techniques, and the latest marketing ideas. I worked at turbo speed and raced past my ninety-day probation into the vice president's seat in what seemed like no time flat. What's more, Jimbo, allowed me to purchase a 33 percent stake in the corporation. Three years after starting, I was twenty-six years old and was making more money than I knew how to spend.

The ascent to vice president and shareholder ranks as some of the best years of my life. Imagine me, a thrill junkie, with access to an entire store of engines. I had died and been reborn in nirvana. Weekends were jammed packed with fun, and they were much too short. We were always taking jaunts with family and friends to nearby lakes for summer jet skiing or winter trips to ski resorts with snowmobiles in tow. And guess what? I was sober.

My parents were ecstatic about the new me. They could hold their heads high after years of hearing whispers about my screw-ups. My mom would say she always knew I had it in me, adding "You only needed the right break."

People in the community, including my close friends, couldn't believe the change. I'd gone from the drunken wild man and someone they thought would be dead before the age of thirty, to a respectable businessman. My friends had college degrees, yet they were still trying get their careers moving, whereas I'd been launched in a major way.

What was most surprising to everyone was the fact I wasn't doing drugs or drinking or misbehaving. It appeared I'd gained a measure of self-control; somehow I'd flipped a switch. As half-baked as I know that idea is today, I actually bought it back then. I thought I was fine. In my mind I'd simply assumed my rightful place at the top of the pile. I was the first of my friends to buy a house. I married the prettiest girl in town. I was running a multimillion-dollar company. I had all the toys. I'd made it.

Admittedly, I got a little full of myself. My old nemesis, ego, had been working overtime. Instead of telling me how big of a loser I was, it was telling me how great I was. And as the old saying goes, pride comes before the fall. I never even saw mine coming.

I'd like to pause for a moment and share some self-analysis. During my three-year climb at Willows, I didn't do anything to address the root of my addiction. I never looked at what drove me into escapism. What happened when I began to achieve success was simply a trade of one addiction for another. I got high on the fast-paced nature of the business, hitting home run after home run. Jimbo loved me, the staff was happy, and customers were grateful. I was in the big leagues, and everyone could see I was doing well. That was extremely important to me, for others to see my success. For a while, it was enough to suppress the desire for substance.

But what happens when you don't pull a weed up by its roots? It keeps growing, getting bigger underneath the soil while above ground everything seems fine.

One day I was sitting in my office and evaluating my kingdom. I was Mr. Big Shot. Think of me in a red wine–colored smoking jacket, pipe in hand, kicked back with my legs crossed. (I'd never wear anything like that, by the way, but you get the point.) Life was good, and I was even better. I patted myself on the back as I mentally replayed the amazing turn of events in my life.

However, while doing so I ran across something I hadn't noticed during the ascent: a black, empty space. I did a double take. *Hold up second. What was that?* I rewound and restarted in slow motion. When I came to the black space, I paused and zoomed in. It was a room filled with dragons I'd not bothered to slay, salivating and waiting to be unleashed.

What had occurred to me, as I sat there swimming in my greatness, was that I didn't have anywhere to go. It dawned on me that my Willows climb was over. There was nothing left for me to conquer.

My very next thought was, *Oh my God, what am I going to do now?* In the next breath my fear came back. It happened that quickly. And what happens when fear grips me? I drink.

At that point I had become what one would call a responsible social drinker. Molly and I would meet friends for dinner, and I'd maybe have a drink or two. At family gatherings I'd have a couple of beers, but it was about being social, and I never got tipsy. But that began to change. Once again drinking was about quelling the fear and the growing noise inside my head. Ego had played a dirty trick and was now reminding me that I was a loser. *You can't hide it anymore. They know...*

Remember the analogy of the weed not being pulled by the root? Well, all of my old fears returned, only they were bigger and stronger. I tried to fight it, but it was like I'd stepped in the quickest quicksand and was going down no matter what. Although I'd never noticed before, I'd catch customers reactions to my eccentric viewing techniques. Before I could explain, the voice would blurt, *They know you're a handicap. They know you're not smart. You're a loser, Charlie.*

Suddenly I could do nothing right. My promotions failed. Sales began to fall. The team appeared discontent. The idea that I wasn't good enough grew into a tsunami, and I started to snort cocaine to feel better. I remember clearly the day I put the straw in my nose. I thought, *Why are you doing this, Charlie? You've got it all, and you know where this is going. You're gonna blow it.*

Cocaine and alcohol made fast work, reclaiming their foothold in my life. I was able to hide it for a while—I was good at that. But the combo of booze and cocaine was like taking body shots from Mike Tyson; eventually I was going to break down. If Molly had ten bucks for every time she had to find me wasted and hunched over in a bar, she could retire. If she wasn't picking me up from a tavern, she was praying I'd wobble home safely on my scooter. Those were good days.

As my frustration grew, I was reminded by my ego that I could *sell* motorcycles, but I wasn't good enough to legally ride them. One can easily guess what happened next. I'd drink, unlock the shop, and joyride recklessly about town, screaming full-throttle at all hours of the night.

As it was bound to happen, one night I was out on an ATV, and the cops got after me. I hightailed it for the store, blasting through red lights and stop signs. I arrived at Willows, hustled inside, killed the lights, and ducked out of sight just as the police showed up. They must have beat on the door for half an hour, but there was no way in hell I was going to answer. I figured if I waited, they'd give up and go eat doughnuts. Well, they didn't—they called Jimbo.

Jimbo knew who I was before he hired me. He was well aware that like him, I'd raised a little—well, actually, a lot of hell around town. But he figured I'd grow out of it. And for three years his gamble paid dividends. I was a model citizen. When he arrived, he smoothed it over with the cops, who knew him as well as they knew me. I don't recall what our follow-up conversation was like, but I'm sure he filed it as a one-time slip.

It wasn't until he started getting complaints from the staff that he knew something was wrong. And boy, was it. I was in the middle of a tornado of cocaine and alcohol abuse, and I couldn't think straight. But of course I didn't think anybody noticed my constant sniffing and frequent trips to the bathroom. Anyone who has witnessed addiction firsthand will understand this picture. Addicts lose the ability to see themselves objectively. Liken it to the anorexic, who looks in the mirror and sees a fat person. Once, Molly and I went to dinner with a childhood friend and his wife. We hadn't seen them in a while, and I was about a year into my slide. He told me some years later that his wife had cried when we left. That's how bad I looked.

Things came to a head after Jimbo returned from a weeklong conference. He'd left me in charge. He told me that according to the staff, I'd spent the majority of the time in the bathroom snorting lines—when I bothered to show up at all. The team was tired of the Charlie Collins Show and encouraged him to make changes. When he confronted me, I denied the whole thing. A man of his worldly experience could see the truth, though. I was clearly in deep trouble.

Life on the home front was spinning out of control just as quickly. Molly, who had demonstrated tremendous love and patience as I fell deeper into addiction, was worried sick. "Charlie, you need to do something. You need help," she would often plead. But I couldn't hear her; the noise in my head was too loud.

And so there I was, two years after my peak at Willows, back in the prison I had built. Drugs and alcohol had me in heavy chains, and I didn't think I would ever be free.

CHAPTER 19

I was heading into my fifth year at Willows when Jimbo finally pulled the plug. By then I'd backed him so far into a corner that he didn't have a choice. To say I'd become a distraction would soft-pedal the havoc that came with the Charles Collins Production. I won't go into details, but imagine trying to work with someone who's strung out on cocaine and alcohol. Do I need to say anymore? I wasn't all that surprised when he sat me down and delivered the news; I'd felt it coming. Even in the midst of the chaos that was my life, there was a silent observer who would speak to me. *You've got to stop, Charlie. You're killing yourself.* It was the same message I'd heard from Molly, echoed by Jimbo and my family as well. But I wasn't nearly ready to take a serious look at the man in the mirror; that would happen much later in my life. However, had I bothered, I would have discovered that the genesis of my self-destruction formed the same day I learned there would be no pill to make my eyes better. Believe it or not, at a place that was many layers deep, it still haunted me. Looking back, the tell was obvious.

I'd gone to outpatient rehab, the first of eight attempts to get clean, during the tail end of my third year at Willows. I finally gave in after incessant pleas from my wife and an ultimatum from Jimbo. It was doomed to fail before I set foot in the door. Rehabilitation, and change in general, happens first in the mind. You have to alter the way you think before altered behavior can follow. In the case of those with addictive patterns—alcohol, food, shopping, gambling, or whatever—I'll go a step further: there has to be a raging desire for new way of being. Take it from a pro: until you reach the point where you can truthfully say, "I will do whatever it takes," you're just going through the motions.

My attitude going into the program wasn't even in the ballpark. I looked at the people around me and thought, *I'm not like anybody here. What the hell am I doing in this place?* Most were hardcore addicts whose physical bodies showed the toll of heavy use. I mean, they *looked* like drug addicts. They looked like losers, like they'd just crawled out of the gutter. And as I saw it, whatever problems they had, it was nothing compared to mine. None of them could claim God had personally cursed them. None of them could say he'd made them a handicap and snatched every dream they'd ever had. My pain was bigger than anyone in that room could know. Nobody could tell me anything about suffering because I owned the patent.

After completing the program, I was no better off than when I'd entered. In fact, I might have gotten worse. The illusion that my suffering was unique gave birth to the idea that I was stronger than the average addict. I could control cravings with my mind, so it wasn't long before I made a call to my connection. From there I began a scenario that I would repeat a few times. I started slow, keeping everything mellow, but eventually my use gained the momentum of a steamroller. And then, for the first time in my life, I suffered severe consequences for my actions. It was a blow to my psyche that came close to taking me over the edge.

My identity was tied to those words *"vice president and shareholder."* They were who I was, or at least how I saw myself. It was as if I'd been stripped naked and made to stand in Times Square. I was so ashamed and vulnerable, and I knew the vultures would come pick at my flesh and laugh in the process. "What a loser," they would say. And sadly, they'd be right. I'd finally done something good in my life. For a solid three years, I'd held my demons at bay and lived a dream. Everybody saw me do it. People told me I was good and smart, and they admired me. My parents were proud and my friends thought well of me. But I blew it. The toughest phone call I ever made was the call to tell Molly, "Jimbo wants me out."

All she said was, "Don't worry about it, honey. We'll figure this out."

It might have hurt less had she screamed, telling me that I was a failure and that she couldn't stand to be with me anymore. Instead she stood strong by my side and never so much as flinched. The day after I walked out of Willows, I checked into a state-run facility to begin my journey of healing. I ended up staying there for five days before moving to a private facility for an additional two weeks.

Prompted by a hard fall from grace, I was forced to take that look in the mirror I'd been avoiding. You've been with me on this ride and understand I'd always come up smelling like roses. Well, landing in the bottom of a barrel, in a no-frills rehabilitation program run by the state of Connecticut, jarred me into reality. Something was wrong with my life—I had a very serious problem. It was during the first week that I accepted my alcoholism and embraced the principles of Alcoholics Anonymous.

I came home after three weeks, and the reality that my life had been turned upside down hit me square in the jaw. I didn't have a job and was back in a familiar place of not being sure what my future held. Other than going to AA meetings, I didn't leave the house for about month. With nothing to do and racked with shame, I sat around in a growing state of mental darkness. I couldn't find a way to forgive myself, and the guilt began to wear on me. I knew I was approaching a cliff when I asked myself, *What do I have to live for?* and found no answer. The idea that I might be better off dead began to cross my mind daily. I can tell you with certainty that had it not been for Molly, I would not be here; the voices that told me I had nothing to live for would have become too strong. But she was so convinced beyond measure that things would work out, and I began to believe. Then one day I noticed a dim light in the distance and stopped looking behind me. Over time, by looking forward, I emerged from my depression.

All along Molly had encouraged me to take my time and figure out what I wanted to do. Once I emerged from the fog, I was able to see that not everything that happened at Willows was bad. In essence, I'd earned a degree from the school of hard knocks. I'd become an expert in retail operations. I knew a ton about sales, marketing, publicity, media, and more. When sober, I was a fantastic leader—leader being the operative word. The vice president and shareholder experience solidified something I'd known since I'd hustled my first driveway job: I was a pure entrepreneur. I simply needed to figure out what my next move would be.

Ideas began to brew, but nothing struck right away. By this time, however, I was ready to get on with my life. I wanted to work—I *needed* to work, for my self-esteem. Work was my faithful tool to rebuild my self-worth. It didn't really matter what the job was; I was willing to do anything. So I went to work for Molly's brother at his gas station.

These days are long past, but if you're old enough, you'll remember the service station attendant, the guy that greeted you in a crisp Dickey uniform and asked with a smile, "Fill 'er up?" And while the gas pumped, he'd check your tire pressure, check the oil, top off your fluids, and clean your windshield. That was me.

Obviously, it was a steep fall from Willows. And it wasn't like I was working in a corner office, either—I was right out there for all of Cheshire to see. There weren't many days when I didn't have to absorb the blow of someone asking, "I thought you owned Willows?" You know my struggles with self-worth. Therefore when I say "humbling" is not a strong enough word to describe the situation, you understand. And, let me make it clear: I wasn't working because we needed the money; Molly had began her career as a social worker and in addition to her salary, which was plenty for us to live comfortably, we had full medical benefits. I was there for me. Therefore I took my lumps and was determined to be the best attendant that had ever lived. As fate would have it, the drive to be the best and to do things better was what led me to start my next business.

Let me quickly set the table before I tell you what happened. If you recall, a dynamic of my work ethic was pursuit of praise. It was especially important at that junction because I was in a rebuilding stage. It was important that customers like my service and tell me as much. And that was easy when they wanted a full tank.

On the other hand, it was next to impossible when they wanted, say, twenty bucks' worth. My problem? I couldn't read the numbers on the pump from a distance. Let me tell you, that makes being the best service station attendant a little difficult. Talk about frustration! Imagine three cars at once, and I'm hustling. I've got hoods up and nozzles going, and I'm working from car to car. It's not like I can glance from underneath a hood and read the pump—I have to get my face within millimeters. After many occasions of dispensing too much fuel, I grew frustrated. I wondered how I could do this simple job better; there had to be another way. Then I thought, *Why is life so hard for people like me? Why can't someone invent something that allows me to read the pump from under the hood? Some kind of implant to go in my eye—a bionic eye? Maybe there's something already out there, and I just don't know about it.* That was possible. I wondered that if something did exist, how would I buy it? They certainly didn't sell that kind of stuff in any store that I'd ever heard of.

In the next moment the skies parted, and down from the heavens came an idea that set me on fire. It was divine inspiration, if nothing else. I went from chaos and not knowing what life held for me in one moment, to knowing exactly what I needed to do.

CHAPTER 20

A store for people like me, for those who lived with visual impairment, those who craved independence, trailblazers in a society designed for the sighted. That's what the world needed.

The idea struck like a temple gong inside my skull and vibrated through my extremities. It was one of those moments that caused me to bang the heel of my hand against my forehead and think, *Duh! Why didn't I think of this earlier? Who better to do this than me? I'm gonna sell magnifiers, CCTVs like the one I'd used at Willows, screen-reading software, large-print books, audio books—the whole shebang.* I didn't have the slightest idea if the store I imagined even existed. I envisioned a place where customers could test-drive products, touch them, feel them, and get educated on real-world use. I'd have it all, anything and everything to make life easier and to foster independence.

I'd been blind all my life and knew for sure there was no such store in my area; it was a safe bet that if there was, George or one of my sisters would have mentioned it to me. I planned to double-check with them later. But first I put on the vice president hat I'd worn at Willows and dove into a market survey. I wanted to get a thirty-thousand-foot view of the landscape before I told anybody about my idea. I began my research with guarded excitement.

I wasn't fifteen minutes in before I felt as alive as I could ever remember. I was tingling! That day, in that very moment, there was a gigantic market waiting to be served. The numbers were off the charts and rising. As you've learned, my disorder is called Stargardt disease, also known as juvenile macular degeneration. With just a little digging,

I learned there were millions of people that lived with age-related eye disorders, and I was shocked. Remember, once I was diagnosed, I'd never bothered to think about anyone other than myself, so the magnitude of what I found was staggering.

There were a number of diseases known to cause legal blindness. However, glaucoma, diabetic retinopathy, and age-related macular degeneration (AMD) were the main culprits. I discovered there were two types of AMD, wet and dry. As I sat at my computer reading the research and dissecting the statistics, my jaw fell. I thought, *How come nobody is talking about this stuff?* It was big news in my book. My goodness, there were millions of Americans suffering. If they'd experienced half the trouble I had, then the world had far too much sadness. A wave of compassion rushed through my veins as I identified and empathized with the collective suffering. It was then that my feet set, and I locked in and got serious. A part of me began to feel like I *had* to open the store. Because my hunch was those affected had no idea that products to make their lives easier even existed, let alone where to buy them. And if they did know, they could be living with the shame I felt of being less-than. Believing that life was over and they had nothing to live for.

I kept digging and knew I was on to something big.

As I plowed deeper into the statistics I discovered an epidemic on the horizon among the baby boomers. It made sense: as we age, our chances for developing eye diseases increase dramatically. I discovered that macular degeneration is the leading cause of blindness for those aged fifty-five and older in the United States. At that time, nobody had a clue as to the cause. That meant preventative measures didn't exist, and millions of people were heading for a meeting with legal blindness.

Then it got a little scary. There was a study that examined the financial burden and the impact on governmental budgets for age-related macular degeneration, cataracts, diabetic retinopathy, and glaucoma. It looked at direct medical costs, other direct costs such as transportation to and from the doctor, and productivity losses. It was estimated the annual total financial burden of major adult visual disorders was $35.4 billion ($16.2 billion in direct medical costs, $11.1

billion in other direct costs, and $8.0 billion in productivity losses)[5]. I whistled long and slow, saying to myself, "That's a lot of money."

When I laid the variables on the table, it looked like a good move. There was a problem of gigantic size and scope; that much was clear. In other words, there were plenty of customers to be had. But that's not all that drove me to pitch the idea to my wife. There is an undeniable psychology that goes along with vision loss, especially for those who experience it later in life. The sudden loss of independence often leads to depression. I knew all about that and figured the story of my journey could be helpful.

I wasn't sure how Molly would react, and so I sort of tiptoed into the conversation. Yes, there was a fire lit inside of me, and yes, I felt an immense calling toward the idea. But I was still licking my wounds from the Willows debacle, and on some level I felt like a failure. However, I think more than anything, I wasn't sure how I would pull it off; it was a bold idea.

So one day I casually said, "I'm thinking about opening a store," and I waited for her reaction.

"What kind of store?" she asked quietly.

"Well, a store with low-vision products. A place where people would be able to come and see the stuff, and learn how to use things the right way. You know, I could teach them."

In true Molly fashion, all she said was, "That sounds nice." And we left it at that.

I walked away having no inkling as to what she thought. But the more I contemplated it, the more my idea grew. Every day a vision of how the store would look, how it would operate, and what kind of products I would carry became more clear. I'd lie in bed at night and see customers in the store smiling, their eyes wide and brimming with hope, the same way I did when I discovered the world of electronic magnification and low-vision devices.

---

[5]   John Wittenborn & David Rein, *Cost of Vision Problems: The Economic Burden of Low Vision and Vision Loss in the United States,* (NORC at the University of Chicago, June 2013)

I shared bits and pieces of my ideas with Molly as they came to me. She was never discouraging and watched my energy grow. And boy, did it grow. To me there's nothing more exciting than living in the creative space, in the land of ideas. I was filled with them. It was like I had a direct link to the universal source of ingenuity. When I sat her down and said, "I'm going to do it. I'm going to open a store," she didn't blink.

She said, "Go for it!"

Next, I decided to call my brother, who by this time had moved to Colorado. I intended to share the news with the whole family, but George was first. He'd always been practical and levelheaded, and he made good choices. It wasn't like anything he may have said would have stopped me from moving forward, though, because my mind was made up. Still, I wanted to hear from him that I wasn't completely off my rocker. It turned out to be a conversation I will never forget. I was selling him on my idea and going over all the research numbers, marketing ideas, and so on. I told him about how I was going to change lives, and how cool it would have been if we'd have known of a store like this.

I finished my spiel and asked, "So, what do you think?"

"That's a great idea," he said. "I think there's a place just like that here in Colorado. I heard they have great products and do a ton of business. You should—"

"What?" I was floored. "Did I hear you say you know of a store where you can buy mags and CCTVs? That's what I thought I heard."

"Apparently there's a place just like what you just described, not far from my house. I hear they've got everything you can think of."

"How come you never told me?"

He said, "You never asked."

I couldn't talk because my brain had kicked into high gear with that bit of good news. I was already planning a trip to go see that store!

One thing I'd learned at Willows was not to reinvent the wheel. I know it sounds cliché, but it's a useful concept. At a minimum, all businesses should begin with a proven model; one can decide to add, subtract, or localize once you understand the working components. I knew that once I saw the concept in action, I would know exactly what steps to take.

Before I could tell George I was coming for a visit, he said, "Maybe you should fly out and meet the owners. They're really nice, I hear—a husband and wife team. You might get some ideas."

I was on my way to Colorado before the week was up, and the experience would forever change my life.

The store was the brainchild of a husband and wife team, Jim and Cindy Misner. They started the business out of frustration when Jim, who was blind, got fed up with having to scour the earth for assistive technology. He recognized the need for a one-stop shop that specialized in products for the blind and visually impaired, and he was right. The store was an instant hit, and when I visited it had been in business, thriving for ten years.

I was rendered speechless when I walked in the door. There were rows and rows of things I recognized: stand and handheld magnifiers in a full array of powers, and several brands of CCTVs. But what raised my excitement to a new level was all the stuff I'd never seen. I'd never seen portable electronic magnifiers that changed contrast and had false colors. That was huge, and I'll tell you why. Most people with vision disorders need high contrast, and they read with white letters on a black background, the inverse of how a sighted person reads. There is another segment of the population that makes use of false colors. They might prefer a blue background with yellow letters or black letters on a red background; it varies from person to person. The idea that I could walk around with a customizable device with such features in my pocket was mind-blowing. I was taking notes as quickly as I could while envisioning what my store would look like. Then Jim introduced me to the world of blindness products, something I hadn't thought of: braille displays, braille embossers, braille paper and computers, digital book players, electronic notetakers, talking watches, screen readers, and different types of text-to-speech software. It was dizzying.

Jim and Cindy were very gracious and told me everything I needed to know to get my business off the ground. As it turned out, their formula for success was identical to what I believed would be my competitive advantage. First, Jim and Cindy were sharp. They could have been successful in the business of jewelry or manufacturing, whatever they chose. However, I thought that Jim's firsthand knowledge of blindness was what made the store hum; it gave their brand a credibility and a trust factor that was hard to match. It made sense that their store was the nation's largest and most well respected retail outlet for vision-related products.

I left Colorado with a clear-cut action plan. Step one was to get my sister Tricia to help me write a business proposal.

CHAPTER 21

In the process of writing the business plan, I fleshed out my ideas and took a deeper look at the numbers. All the research pointed at the low-vision industry being an emerging niche market. The convergence of clinical research, a clever repurposing of electronic technology (flat panel monitors being one example), and people who desperately needed it were the driving forces. With business plan in hand, I sauntered into the bank looking for a loan.

I'll pause here for a quick lesson for my fellow entrepreneurs, or those of you who've been sitting on an idea but are afraid to move. As I think back on my business career, there have been two critical ingredients that have seen me through: confidence and enthusiasm. It seems that if you have those qualities, everything else will work itself out along the way. Doug Larson said the following, and it's so true: "Some of the world's greatest feats were accomplished by people not smart enough to know they were impossible." That was me when I walked into the bank.

It could be said that I was on the leading edge of a movement—which, by the way, has evolved into a multimillion-dollar global industry. But at the time, no one had even heard of low-vision—in fact, I don't think the term had even been coined. People like me were simply called "legally blind." I'm guessing whoever made the call did it for the sighted world. Remember, most people don't understand vision impairment; they think a person can see or can't. Saying our vision is low connotes sight but not very good sight.

It wouldn't have mattered what industry jargon was used when I walked in that bank. I was so fired up, so confident with my idea, that the banker couldn't help but give me a loan. It didn't matter that he didn't understand the market, because he was certain I did. There wasn't an industry to compare my financial projections, but so what? The gusto with which I told my story captivated him. I explained how there were millions of people suffering, many of them in close proximity, who had no idea there was help waiting for them. I told him how my store would meet those needs, answer questions, and provide the right products. My store would help people live again! I knew this to be true because I had lived it.

I got the loan: a little over one hundred thousand dollars.

Combined with my life savings, I had about $140,000 to launch what I was going to call Vision Dynamics. There's a great story about how the name Vision Dynamics came to be.

At this point in my life, I was still very much led by ego. I didn't know it, of course, but I was. And that meant the business needed my name—in the biggest, brightest, boldest signage possible. The world needed to know that Charlie had a store and that he was doing well. Right? I can't tell you how many versions of "Charlie" and "Charles" and "Collins" got mixed with the words "vision" and "sight" and "eyes." I was at my wits' end, and I couldn't seem to find a combination that resonated. For inspiration, Molly, who is a wonderful artist, sketched a beautiful drawing of an eye with long, flowing lashes that a supermodel would envy. I would stare at the drawing with head tilted and brows furrowed, scratching my temple, hamstrung and irritated that nothing seemed to work.

This went on for a few weeks, until one day I was talking with my brother-in-law, Peter, and the name came to me out of the blue. I was telling him about the industry and my plans for the store in typical Charlie fashion: passionate, convincing, self-assured. "But I'm not sure what to call it," I finished with a tinge of frustration.

I continued to tell him about all the stuff I'd seen in Colorado. I told him how different things were from when I had been first diagnosed. "And it's only getting better," I said. "The products they have now are amazing. People are going to flip when they see this stuff. I think I'm on to something."

With a chuckle Peter said, "Well, since you are the most dynamic person I've ever met, it's gonna work."

The world paused in an instant of absolute, quiet clarity. In that moment a thousand thoughts ricocheted through the coils of our collective brains. In unison and in a reverent whisper, we both said, "Vision Dynamics."

I'd gotten a loan, the name had been gifted to me by the universe, and now all I needed then was to find a location. Based on my personal struggles, I knew there were a few things that were nonnegotiable. I'm going to take the long route to explain what they were, so stay with me.

My trip to Colorado had solidified and broadened the marketing idea I'd been playing with from the start. I was going to use my life as an example, as a selling point. Like Jim, I would be the living, breathing version of what I intended to market: independence and self-reliance. If this was true, then I would need to embody the concept. In order to do that, I had to finally embrace that I was legally blind. So, I did—kind of. Actually, what I did was take in enough of it to get the store moving.

I was going to preach independence. That meant the location of the store had to foster self-sufficiency for both myself and my customers. For me, I needed a place that was close to home so that I could either walk or ride my scooter. For local customers, it needed to be near public transportation—a bus line or a train stop. I also wanted it to be centrally located in the state; I had visions of people driving from the furthest reaches of Connecticut once they heard the good news. I imagined busloads making day trips from Maine, Massachusetts, and New Hampshire, too. With this vision in the forefront of my thoughts, the perfect location magically appeared. I found a commercial space right on the bus line, 3.5 miles from my house, and dead center in the state. I secured a lease and prepared to open the doors to my dream.

CHAPTER 22

My new friends in Jim and Cindy had agreed to sell me products to get Vision Dynamics off the ground. I called them up and ordered forty thousand dollars' worth of inventory: magnifiers, desktop CCTVs, magnification software, lighting, large-print keyboards. I went crazy. I wanted my store to carry anything and everything I'd ever wanted. Not only did I buy devices, but also I purchased what we now call DLAs, Daily Living Aids. DLAs include talking watches, large-print books, and check-writing guides, to name a few. For those of you in the sighted world, I'll use a two-dollar check-writing guide to illustrate its immeasurable value.

Remember the pre-electronic payment days—that prehistoric time when people actually wrote checks to pay bills or buy things? Now imagine the cable bill is past due, and the Super Bowl (or some equivalent) is on Sunday. It is imperative you get that check in the mail right away, or you'll be watching the game with your in-laws, who chafe you like a dull razor. The only problem is you can't distinguish the payment line from the date line or the signature line; it's all one big blur. How would you handle it? Would you guess? Would you wait for your loved one's help, again? Lots of people become so frustrated that they give up on signing checks altogether. Well, something as simple as a check-writing guide solves the problem. It's a template you overlay on a checkbook that frames the lines. All you do is write inside the boxes and keep your dignity (and sanity).

I spent another twenty thousand dollars on shelving, display cases, light fixtures, wall mounts, and my point of sale (POS) system. And remember, I wasn't a novice at retail business operations; on the contrary, I was a bit of an expert. Vision Dynamics was going to be my dream setup. Everything was going to be perfectly designed to make my life easy. The POS system would be low-vision friendly, with large-print keyboards loaded with magnification software. The store would be well lit, and items were marked with large-print, high-contrast signage. The setup was conceived out of my frustrations at the ski shop, my successes at Willows, and dreams of what I always wished I'd had.

Soon, what seemed like a never-ending stream of boxes began to arrive. I recall standing in the midst of them all and thinking, *Holy crap! This is going to be a ton of work.*

Undaunted, I began the task of setting up my store. My dream was coming to life. I cleared some space in the center of the room, dragged out the first display case, and went about putting it together. My vision impairment notwithstanding, I'm good at putting things together. I'm handy with tools and don't need instructions to know how things fit. Even still, it must have taken me three grueling hours to finish the first display. I took a box count, multiplied the hours, and realized I was in over my head. *This is going to take forever if I don't get some help.*

I picked up the phone and called my dad. Little did I know that it would begin what has turned into a sixteen-year journey we've taken together. To say the time was perfect for us to join forces would deny the God-force its credit. My dad was essentially retired; all of the kids had left home, and he was working part time at a computer store. It just so happened that the store went out of business, and I called him the next week. As my story moves, on you'll understand why this turned out to be the kind of circumstances only the Creator orchestrates.

I said, "Hey, Dad, um… What are you doing right now?"

"Nothing really," he answered.

"You want to come by and give me a hand in the store? I'm putting together a bunch of display cases and could use your help."

"I guess I could do that," he said. "I'll be over in an hour."

We knocked out three cases in the time it would have taken me to complete one. As we stood admiring our handiwork at the end of the day, I asked, "Hey, would you like to come back tomorrow?"

He did. And he kept coming, helping me step by step to construct my dream. I don't know how I would have pulled it off without him. I knew motorcycles, ATVs, and watercraft, not power saws, wood, and nails. Over time he became as enthusiastic about the store as I was. Besides one little setback, our relationship was perfect.

It turns out I am very much like my dad. I can be short—and I don't mean my height of five foot eight. I could be easily frustrated, just like Dad. I recall how quickly things went sour when he tried to help me with my homework. When ideas or concepts didn't take hold right away, he quickly lost his patience. Well, we had a few of those moments while building the store, only in reverse. I don't remember the details of what happened, but I can tell you that in my egocentric world, everyone was there to meet *my* needs. And of course, when someone fell short, I had to let the person know about it.

My dad didn't hesitate to sit me down and let it be known he wasn't going to tolerate my Prince Charlie attitude. He said, "I don't know if this is going to work out. If you can't control your temper, I'd rather not be here."

I realized how badly I needed him, and I kicked into sales mode. I promised to control my frustration and said that everything was going to be great, and I sincerely meant it. But I must tell you, the part of me that remembered him kicking over the woodpile and those brutal homework sessions almost blurted, "Now you know what it feels like, huh, Dad?" With a loving smile, of course.

It wasn't long before we had the store all set up, and I really loved it. The vision of my mind's eye had become reality, and it gave me this overwhelming sense that I had done the right thing. I had found my way home, so to speak. And then one morning I woke up and recall thinking, *I haven't thought about a drink in... wow, I can't even remember...*

After rehab I'd gotten serious about sobriety and was living the twelve steps of Alcoholics Anonymous. I regularly went to meetings and had a sponsor. I did what I was supposed to do and stayed sober. It wasn't hard because I was so focused on building Vision Dynamics; I'd completely forgotten about anything other than making the store live and breathe. Every day I woke with a singular purpose: opening my store so that I could help people. I was inspired and seemed to have found my true vocation. Around me life was a perfect spring day. My wife was happy as I settled into my sobriety, and our marriage began to heal. My relationship with my father also improved, and it was just as good or better with my mom.

I decided to have a soft opening, to make sure all systems were in order before we went live. I tapped into what I'd learned at Willows and sent out press releases to the local newspapers. Lo and behold, I got a bite. The *Waterbury Republican* came out and did a really nice article with a front-page photo. I still have the picture of me and my dad sitting together inside the store. The article talked about my struggles with vision, featured some of the products, and gave the date and time we would open. It was a sign of things to come.

I believed in the Vision Dynamics concept. I'd seen the concept work in Colorado. Even still you never know what might happen. I've since learned small business owners live in a perpetual state of worry... Mine was, *what if nobody shows up?* I didn't sleep a wink the night before I opened the doors for the first time.

I arrived at the store a few hours before the bell was set to ring. There were some final touches to be completed, but mostly I was pacing, fussing, and re-fussing with details. Moments before we were set to open I'd worked myself into I high-strung nervous mess.

Then finally it was time.

I unlocked the doors, and lo and behold people started showing up. One, then two, then a carload, then a few more. Before I knew it, we had a full house and the place was cooking. I was shocked. Really, I was. I expected a few people would come, but it was much more active than I could have hoped. I ran around the store explaining how products worked, ringing up sales with ease on my low-vision-friendly system. After about ten transactions, I started to grin and thought, *Oh. My. God. I'm going to be rich.*

I remember quite clearly the customer that put it all together for me. She spent close to four thousand dollars with a smile on her face. She was so delighted to realize she could read again, it brought tears to her eyes. She said, "I had no idea these products even existed. How come my doctor never told me?"

When the doors finally closed, I collapsed into a chair, exhausted, but I was smiling. I knew I'd created the perfect scenario. Vision Dynamics was a business that would allow me to help people who suffered like I did. At the same time, I could make a good living doing it. I was on my way.

CHAPTER 23

The grand opening of Vision Dynamics ranks in the top five proudest moments of my life; my wedding day and the birth of my daughters get the highest marks. However, the official launch of a dream is special in a way of its own. As it turns out, it's like getting married and having children all on the same day. Anyone who's ever opened a retail business will understand what I'm talking about.

Dovetailing off the soft launch, I sent out more press releases announcing our official opening. I hit every media outlet in a fifty-mile radius, including the local television stations. I sent letters to doctors and to government officials. I told friends, who told friends, who told friends. I could feel the momentum building as we inched toward opening day. Everything was aligning perfectly—so much so that I couldn't get my arms around the good fortune. When I got confirmation that two of the network TV stations would send crews and that the mayor of Cheshire would attend, I pinched myself to make sure I wasn't dreaming. Not yet understanding the universal forces moving in my life, I assumed I was the luckiest guy in the world.

The day came, and let me tell you, Hollywood could not have scripted a better opening party. In front of my wife (who was pregnant with our first child), my parents, my siblings, and my friends going all the way back to high school, the mayor cut a ribbon in front of my store with a pair of those giant scissors. Then she congratulated me, and everyone saw it. I can't even explain how good that made me feel, and the night only got better. The pats on the back were nonstop as everyone talked about how great an idea it was to open the store. Of course, that meant I was smart and well respected once again. I was a celebrity in high demand that night. *All those people who thought I'd never amount to anything, and everyone who laughed when I got booted out of Willows—well, look at me now,* I thought. Charlie Collins had made something of himself and was doing well. If they weren't there to see it with their own eyes, they'd certainly hear about it, maybe even see it on the news, because there were two news crews with cameras and bright lights, interviewing people. They even interviewed my brother-in-law Peter, whose eyes were perfectly fine. They happened to catch him in a pair of funky reading glasses: heavy-duty black frames with glass thicker than two coke bottles; they looked like you could perform X-rays on the spot. The reporter asked, "So, how do you like your glasses, sir?"

He grinned like the cat that ate the canary and said, "Oh, man, these things are awesome!"

There were food and drinks and laughter, and most of all customers—lots of them. The place was buzzing like a blockbuster film premiere. People bought products left and right, and it was hard for me to keep up. I would be demonstrating one device when someone else would shove through and ask, "How does this thing work?"

When it was all said and done, I'd made over four thousand dollars! I was astounded. Like I said, I suspected the concept would work. Nevertheless, it was a vision, a dream if you will. Holding that money in my hand was concrete, tangible. A dream had turned into reality. When I extrapolated the numbers forward, all I could do was giggle. Charlie Collins was back, big time! I was triumphant like the last scene of a Disney movie. A local boy did good; it was a "return of the prodigal son" kind of tale…

CHAPTER 24

Vision Dynamics took off like a rocket. The business soared beyond my wildest dreams, bigger and faster than I could have ever imagined. It was almost as if it had been sitting on the launch pad with engines idling, waiting for me to get behind the wheel and say, "Let's go!" It was an instant success. Looking back, I can tell you it was a combination of two variables. First, we were the only game in town, which is always a plus. It was a new concept in an emerging market, and my timing could not have been better. Mix in reason number two, my concoction of truth, omissions, slight reshaping of past events, and voila!—the Vision Dynamics story, which in essence was the Charlie Collins story, was compelling. It was Lifetime movie worthy and attracted people to the store in droves.

In a nutshell, this was my pitch: I was someone who had struggled with juvenile macular degeneration since grade school. And boy, did I suffer. I had low self-esteem, feelings of inferiority and depression, and I was on the verge of suicide. Then I accepted my eye disease. Once I truly embraced who I was, my life began to change, and I built myself up, brick by brick, and became a successful businessman. No longer hindered by self-doubt, I'd built a multimillion-dollar corporation. With passion, conviction, and gravitas, I would say, "If I can do it, anybody can!" And of course I meant it. I mean, it was true.

"But you know, selling motorcycles just wasn't enough for me," I would say. "Yes, I was making great money and all, but something was missing. Deep down inside, I knew there was something else I should be doing. You know the feeling I'm talking about?" I would ask my audience, and they would nod in agreement.

"Then one day it hit me. I woke up knowing I needed to help people who suffered as I once did. And the best way to do it was to open Vision Dynamics!"

Customers were moved by the core-truth in my story. Newly blind, they empathized and connected to the fear that walks side-by-side with vision loss. It clicked like an *ah-ha* moment. Vision Dynamics was born of pain and yet it was an agent of hope. It represented a paradigm shift. It was going to make the world a better place.

But there was a little-bitty problem with my story that in the end would loom humongous.

You know from taking this journey the real reasons why I left Willows. I smoked, drank, and snorted my way out the door. But there's no way I could say all that. As bad as I wanted to tell people the true depths of which I had fallen I wouldn't dare. Oh no, not in a million years. They wouldn't think well of me if I did.

Do you sense a miniscule problem brewing here? Do you sense something's wrong with the picture? Something feel not quite right?

Well, it was. My old friend fear was bubbling just beneath the surface—the same brand that I'd felt in my third-grade classroom when asked to read aloud. It was dormant, blanketed by a weakening twelve-step commitment and by the beginnings of monetary success, but it would soon rear its ugly head bigger than ever.

I said earlier that fear seemed coded in my DNA. Don't get me wrong, I understand that all of us deal with insecurities on some level. It just seemed like I'd somehow got an extra-large dose and the added bonus of a companion voice to go with it. An orator sits ear level on my shoulder and whispers when the world is quiet, and it's never been good. There are constant reminders that I'm less than, and that people won't like me. It's a heavy burden to carry, and if I'm not careful, I'm subject to a permanent state of worry. *What will people think of me?* is a thought that's never far away.

It's something that I had to overcome in order to share my story— the truth—with you. As I move closer to the deepest, darkest part of my narrative, please keep in mind that I'm scared and nervous. I'm vulnerable, and the voice is at work: *Oh, they're really going to think you're a loser, Charlie.*

I worry that my life, my story told in uncut, raw, naked truth, could have a negative effect on my family. My daughters are teenagers, and their world can be cold and hard as stone. The last thing I'd want is to see them mocked at school or hounded on Facebook because of the sins of their father. And of course I'm concerned for my wife; I pray she will not be judged for sticking with me when most would have bailed. That would hurt more than you can imagine. Even still, I am going to keep writing. I'm compelled to share it all, in spite of fear. Something tells me that the fire I've gone through was only so that I can inspire those who are still in the furnace and trying to find their way.

As I struggled with this idea, I sought opinions from friends. A person whom I respect said, "You've lived your whole life in fear, worrying about what people might think of you. Come on, Charlie, it's time for it to stop. What a shame it would be to come all this way and not tell the truth. The part you leave out might be the part that helps someone off the ledge. That is why you're writing the book, right? To help people?"

All I could do was say, "Yes."

So before I move on to the roaring success I experienced with Vision Dynamics and the darkness that followed, I'll share something I've learned along the way. Compassion and forgiveness start at home. Until you can look in the mirror and love yourself, no matter what road you've traveled, there's more work to be done. Nobody's perfect, right? Everyone has fallen short because that's what we humans do. But thank God that life is not about falling—it's about getting up, about the willingness to stand, dust off, and keep trying.

CHAPTER 25

I mentioned that the store took off as if shot from a cannon. To give you a little perspective on just how quickly, get this: Vision Dynamics opened its doors in October 1997, and by year's end it had churned gross revenues of nearly three hundred thousand dollars! That was a helluva launch for a brand-new retail business, and as it turned out, it was an omen for the success to come. The next year we doubled our revenue *and* turned a healthy profit. Products flew off the shelves so quickly that I could hardly keep up. The next year we doubled sales again and netted even more profit. In a relativity short time, Vision Dynamics had gained a reputation as the go-to place in New England for low-vision devices. Customers travelled from all over the region. Then, believe it or not, we doubled revenues again.

I once heard a basketball player try to describe an incredible shooting performance, one of the nights when everything he threw up went in. He shrugged and said, "I don't know. The rim was as big as a hula-hoop tonight." That's what the initial run of Vision Dynamics was like for me. I was in the zone, inspired and connected to something bigger than myself. I had the Midas touch. Ideas fell from Heaven, and 99 percent of them worked. It wasn't long before CCTV, magnifier, and other device manufacturers were beating down my door hoping to earn my loyalty. Vision Dynamics (Charlie Collins) was being courted like the pretty girl at the dance. And man, did I bathe in it. I was important, and people thought well of me.

I secured contracts with local nonprofits, state agencies throughout New England, and a big fish: the Veterans Administration. The VA is the largest purchaser of low-vision devices in the world; the biggest group of visually impaired are veterans of Vietnam. However, there are a rising number of soldiers returning from wars abroad with a variety of trauma-related vision impairments.

It wasn't long before word of my miraculous journey of survival began to spread. People wanted to hear from the horse's mouth how I got electrocuted by a train and lived. They wanted to know about my late-night escapades behind the wheel. They wanted to understand the loathing self-hatred that nearly killed me. Mostly, however, they connected with a refusal to accept an eye disorder and question God's judgment. Remember, most of my clients suffered from age-related disorders and were dealing with a "new normal." I knew what it was like to wonder, *Why is this happening to me?* My story gave them hope, and so I began to hone my public speaking skills.

Remember that kid in third grade who was afraid to stand in front of the class? Slowly but surely, he gave way to a new kid who realized he had something to say that people wanted to hear. And of course, it didn't hurt that I happened to be talking about my favorite subject. The next thing I knew, I was promoting Vision Dynamics (Charlie Collins) with the fervor of an evangelist. I learned to captivate my audiences with high drama and humor. One could hear a pin drop when I spoke. Life was very good indeed.

I hadn't had a drink since I'd gotten out of rehab, post-Willows. I know you've heard this before, but drinking didn't cross my mind. I'm guessing you find that rather odd? How could someone go from craving alcohol and drugs to not even thinking about it? I've invested a tremendous amount of effort in understanding how *my* brain works, and here's *my* deal. In the simplest terms, I have a gigantic void. If you think of my void as a living, breathing animal that constantly needs to be fed, then you can begin to understand my daily challenge. I didn't think about alcohol or drugs because I was getting high on Vision Dynamics and was making some serious coin. The accolades from family and friends were nonstop. I enjoyed a near rock star status around town. People knew of me, and they knew I was doing well. I was pretty hard to miss, given that I was a constant in the news with front-page articles and TV features—the local expert on the budding epidemic of low vision. My void was enjoying ice cream and cake, and the more money I made, the fewer AA meetings I attended.

In my mind I really didn't need the meetings; I was too important to be sitting around with a bunch of failures. I had a business that was thriving, and I was an upstanding member of the community. Meetings were not a good use of my very valuable time. When I did make time, it was just to remind those weak-minded failures that I was an example of what they could be if they tried hard enough.

Life was beyond good.

In 2000 Molly and I had our second baby. By that time the store was doing so well that we purchased our second home. Molly quit her job and stayed home with our infant and two-year-old on full-time mommy duty. Everything had finally aligned and come together perfectly. I was living in my dream home: five bedrooms and four full bathrooms, sitting on three acres and, nestled in the woods. I could do whatever I wanted because I had the financial means. One day I decided we needed new windows, so I wrote a check. I didn't have to plan or get financing—I just did it. I thought we needed a new sprinkler system, so I dug up the yard and went state-of-the-art. I bought a new roof. It was nothing for me to drop hundreds of dollars on Grateful Dead CDs. Of course, I needed a high-end system to crank Jerry, so I went out and dropped fifteen thousand on a stereo system. I owned a sports car I couldn't drive, ATVs, a sweet Italian scooter, and a boat. If you looked at my life from the outside, you'd think, *God, does that guy have it made. Beautiful wife, daughters that are absolute dolls, a thriving business, and all the goodies.*

But really, I was as empty as I had ever been, and in quiet moments the voice would arrest me, wake me as if cold bucket ice had been dumped on my crown. *You're not good enough, Charlie. Everyone knows it. They can see your life is a lie.*

At first my answer was to run down my checklist. I'd think, *Hey, wait a minute! That can't be true. I've got a beautiful family. A house. I've got money. All the toys I could ever want. I've got a great business. There's no way I'm depressed.*

I kept right on marching, not knowing I was heading for a dead end.

CHAPTER 26

Early on in my story, I talked about Hotchkiss Grove being the place where I fell in love with boating. It was there that the sensation of gliding along on the ocean became one of my biggest pleasures. The sea, or any body of water for that matter, has a magical quality that moves me. Time appears to shape-shift. I know that it's passing by the movement of the sun, but it doesn't have the same linear feel as when I'm on land. It has an empyrean quality—celestial, if you will. I'm present, engaged, and in tune with the God-force of the wind, the heavens, and the churning sea. It's every bit as good as church, if you ask me. A connection to God is a connection to God, and no matter how it comes, it feels good. Of course, I didn't understand any of this when I bought my first boat in 1998: a twenty-five-foot sailboat. All I knew was that business was good, I could afford it, and something called me to be on the water.

It wasn't the best boat in the world. It was an old, rickety Cape Dory that I bought off a buddy for a few thousand bucks. But I did what I do: rolled up my sleeves and fixed it up. Every spare moment was spent either on the water or at the marina working to make the boat something of which I could be proud. By the time I finished, people were asking, "Wow! Where did you get that?"

And guess who was by my side every step of the way? The same guy who taught me to sail, the same guy who helped me get Vision Dynamics off the ground: my dad. In the process, our relationship grew into something I would have never imagined. At times I would pause and watch him, thinking, *Is this the same person who kicked over my woodpiles?*

I have to say this period ranks among the most interesting times in my life. My marriage had healed. It seemed as if I had alcohol licked. And clearly, under my leadership Vision Dynamics would be an industry juggernaut. Looking into the future, it was easy to see all of my dreams were within reach. I was in a place I'd never been before; I felt powerful and in complete control of my life. Naturally, the success led me into a new social realm, and with this new place came a new set of friends who had financial means like the ones I began to socialize with at the marina.

Vision Dynamics was clicking on all cylinders and continued to soar. Because money wasn't a problem, I decided it was time to buy a bigger, even better boat. I stepped up and purchased a twenty-eight-foot motorboat. Man, was that baby nice. Everyone was impressed with what they saw, and for good reason. If you think about the checklist for success, I had it nailed.

- Loving wife? Check
- Beautiful kids? Check.
- Comfortable home? Check

My life was complete and utterly amazing, and the money just kept coming. As a result, we'd moved up the social ladder a couple of rungs down at the marina. I didn't have nearly as much as most of my new boating friends, but I still had a pretty awesome lifestyle. I'd strut down the marina, smile, and wave, secretly thinking I'd be looking down on them from the top of the world in a few years. *Enjoy it now, pal, because Charlie Collins is on the move.* I was that young titan on the rise: young, brash, cocky, ambitious, and focused. He's not quite there yet, but everyone knows he's going to make something of himself because his eyes are full of fire.

Social comparison theory was first proposed by social psychologist Leon Festinger in 1954. The idea is centered on the belief that there is a drive within us to gain accurate self-evaluations, and we do this by comparing ourselves to others. His theory was further developed to include downward social comparison and even upward social comparison. I'm sure at some point someone will think of sideways comparison, backward comparison, and comparison-to-comparison. I'm telling you this because my life was already falling apart, and I didn't know it. Today, one of the indicators that I monitor closely is comparing myself to others. When that begins, I know trouble is not far away. Yes, yours truly was and still is a textbook case of someone whose world spins in a state of constant comparison. The only difference between today and life back then is that I have tools; I know how to keep the narrative from leading me to a negative end.

As I climbed socially, my ego swelled commensurately. I began to think of my old friends as not quite as good as me—downward social comparison. It's difficult to admit because if forces me to remember that I wasn't a very good friend at times. Don't we all hate the people who make it big and forget where they came from? Don't we secretly wish for their fall? I'm sure there were lots of people around town who couldn't wait for me to come tumbling off the throne I'd built. In my defense, I was sick and didn't understand the nature of my illness. What I was doing was a defense mechanism, another form of fear. We've all used it at one time or another to dissociate ourselves from a person or group in order to make ourselves feel better. It's only natural when you're empty inside and are looking for anything that will allow you to anchor your self-esteem.

Nevertheless, it remained a fact: my uppity, egotistical attitude drove the people around me crazy. If you were one of those whom I wronged, please accept my apology and a confession that might make you feel better. At the same time I was driving you nuts, I was beginning to drive myself even nuttier.

I was hanging out with people who had much more money than I did. They had bigger, nicer, and newer boats. They had all the bells and whistles, and their boats shined in a way mine didn't. I wasn't aware enough to notice the exact moment the seeds of discontent sprouted. What I do remember was thinking, *I need a new boat.*

And that's what I did. I went all-in and upped the ante in a major way. I bought a top-of-the-line, fully loaded, thirty-one-foot Mainship Sedan Bridge. That boat was ridiculously nice. Two staterooms, full galley with all the appliances, dinette, heating, air-conditioning, whiz-bang electronics, and the biggest motor available, twin 454 7.4-liter V8s with close to 800 horsepower. It made a big-time statement and did all the talking for me. All I had to do was bring my friends aboard, and they would see for themselves that I was doing well.

The feeling of accomplishment didn't last very long. The comparisons started, and I ended right where I'd left off: sitting on the bridge of my top-of-the-line dreamboat and thinking, *This isn't good enough. I need a new boat.*

Only this time I couldn't just go out and buy it—not at that moment. That fact began to wear on my self-worth. As crazy as it sounds, I'd watch the other boat owners out the corner of my eye and knew they were thinking about me: *Look at him, his boat's a pile of crap. Haha! Who does he think he's fooling?* Amazing, isn't it? Today, I look back at that time with a nervous chuckle. It's scary to think how my mind morphed a life of beauty and promise into a raging nightmare. But I managed to do it in grand fashion.

I'd stopped going to AA meetings altogether by this time. I was completely disconnected from God—the internal beacon of truth and honesty—and my identity was rooted further and deeper in the external. That gigantic hunk of plastic slowly and insidiously became a major factor in my identity, and because I couldn't afford a new one, I developed what I would call a psychosis about caring for the boat I had. I spent endless hours washing, waxing, polishing, cleaning, brushing, and swabbing every inch. When I say every inch, I mean it literally. It was insane. The engine compartment was cleaner than most people's kitchens—not a grease spot to be found anywhere. I went through it with a toothbrush. It wasn't borderline obsessive, it was full-blown crazy-man obsessive. Everything had to be perfect or else somebody would notice.

I'd come in off a family day on the water, and I'd get right to work. At first Molly hung around waiting for me to finish. After a while she'd kiss me and say, "See you later." I'd shine and polish until the sun went down, sleep on the boat, wake up, and get right back to work. It got to the point where the other boat owners would jokingly say, "You've gotta stop! You're making me look bad." But I never did—I couldn't. The old feeling that something was wrong had arrived, the inkling that I didn't really belong. And so I began to keep company with discontent on a regular basis.

CHAPTER 27

Imagine me sitting on the bridge of my boat, awash in utopian midday sun. Water lapped gently against the hull, cultivating a meditative state. The smell of fresh caught Atlantic salmon and grilled vegetables floated on a gentle wind. Grateful Dead melodies cranked on my high-end stereo system. Laughter was in the air as my wife, parents, in-laws, sister, and friends enjoyed the fruits of my labor. It was a perfect, storybook afternoon. It was one of those days where someone might pinch themselves to make sure it was real.

Yet I sat behind sunglasses, teeth clenched so tightly the muscles in my jaw flexed. My hands were balled into fists, my foot tapped nervously out of control, and I thought, *Man, does this friggin' suck...*

That moment was a clear and certain demarcation point. It was the day I finally said aloud what had been swirling in my head like far-off voices in the wind. My life sucked, as I saw it. That was my reality, and the curtain raised on a new chapter in my life.

I'm sure that along the path Molly and those close to me felt a shifting of my attitude. I could feel it, too—a daily brick stacked on each shoulder; a corset cinched just a little tighter—but I didn't have a clue as to what was bothering me. If I feel even the tiniest brush of these symptoms today, I know *exactly* what to do: it would be shut-down time; into deep meditation I'd go, sitting quietly until I understood *exactly* what was bothering me.

Back then I didn't have tools. And even if I did, I didn't truly understand the nature of my illness. I was like the woman in the tale of the Princess and the Pea. A woman who claims to be a princess sleeps on a bed covered by twenty mattresses and twenty featherbeds. Hiding in this stack of luxury is a tiny pea that gave her a fitful night of sleep; she even claimed it bruised her. Our lives—the job, the kids, the bills, the this-and-that—can be like those large stacks of bedding: underneath, pea-sized, nagging issues leave us constantly uncomfortable. We know something's wrong, but rather than dig for answers, we have another latte and watch reality television. Well, I can't afford to check out. None of us can. How many times have you heard someone say, "My goodness, I have no idea where the extra ten pounds came from. I looked up, and there they were." That's what happens when you sleep on peas and ignore the pain.

I didn't understand the emergency brewing and kept moving. I fully intended to power through the dark period by the strength of my will, but stuff kept piling up. The emotional twisting in my gut was constant. The voice in my ear was no longer whispering in quiet moments. Oh no, he didn't need quiet moments anymore—he would bust in the door whenever he felt like it and announce, *Charlie, you are a loser.* The roller coaster that was my life had reached another peak and was about plunge furiously into the abyss.

I'd created the perfect storm for failure. If someone came to me and said, "Charlie, I want you to give me the best scenario to destroy your life," I wouldn't have to think twice. First, I'd fueled my so-called happiness by feeding my ego. On the other side of my ego coin was a flippant level of respect for the monster that lived inside of me. I behaved as if my collapse at Willows never happened. I mistakenly believed I had everything under control. The grandest miscalculation of all, however, was not going to AA meetings and helping others. *That* was a bad move and was downright reckless. I will never again underestimate the value of camaraderie, the spiritual fine-tuning that occurs when we lend a hand to those in need, as well as the power of openly admitting, *My name is Charlie, and I'm an alcoholic.*

My thoughts began to spin faster than I could control. Familiar feelings of despair came to life. To give you a picture, I present a snapshot of Charlie Collins's mind, circa 2003. One day I might ask myself that age-old question, *Who am I? What am I doing here on earth?*

I imagine this is something everyone has wondered at one time or another. It is an amazing tool for self-discovery, opening up doors one may not have realized were there.

I never got a chance to ponder the question introspectively, because in a nanosecond, the voice of fear would answer, *You're a friggin' loser—that's who you are. You always have been. Everybody knows it, so why don't you stop pretending?*

Those thoughts were especially strong when it came to my boat, the marina, and the friends I had made there. It got to the point that I couldn't find the solace that the water once offered. The angst would begin to build with just a thought of the marina. As soon as I arrived, the voice would kick into high gear. *Look around: everyone is doing better than you. You don't belong here.* It would twist my gut into knots.

I began to grow angry at and immensely jealous of anybody who was doing better than me. There were lots of them at the marina, and I was the worst kind of jealous. I was the guy who smiled to their faces and secretly wanted to be in their position. I became obsessed with status and couldn't shake the disturbance in my head. I had to do something to feel better, and I knew how to pull it off: all I needed was a bigger boat. Yep, that was it, *I need a bigger boat,* I thought. *Then they will think well of me. They'll see I'm not a loser.*

For my entire life, external stimuli had been my answer to internal problems. I didn't know any better, so naturally I thought bigger, finer, higher quality, and more of it was the answer. At that moment, I felt my entire life needed a sweeping change. Not only did I need a bigger boat, but I needed a bigger house, a faster car (that I couldn't even drive), and a better stereo—more, more, more. I needed to go big, huge, and gigantic!

There was a slight problem, however. Vision Dynamics had plateaued. While my back was turned, somebody cranked shut the money spigot, and it had rusted. Over the course of four years, the industry had grown more competitive. We weren't the only game in town anymore, and certainly not in the region. The niche was no longer a secret, and it seemed entrepreneurs were coming into the industry every week. Today I know this as truth: the low-vision industry had become and remains as competitive as any industry one could name. Don't let the fact that we mostly sell to little old ladies fool you—in the background there's war going on. Back then, though, I didn't have a clue. I didn't think to analyze the market, adjust my messaging, or alter my strategy. Why would I? Everything I'd ever done worked like magic, so I kept doing everything I had been doing, only I did it harder, faster, and longer. Then I'd sit scratching my head when nothing happened. I hired a sales team and had them pound the pavement like Roman soldiers; still the needle wouldn't move. I had my contracts department scouring the country, the world, for opportunities; all they found were small fish, and I needed a whale if I was going to show people that I wasn't less than. Nothing was working, and I slowly became that irrational, irritable, impossible-to-please boss. Hopefully you've never had to personally endure the lunacy I brought to work every day.

In my mind, the problem was simple: people *obviously* were not working hard enough. And if they weren't going to work to please me, to help get me that boat I wanted, then their lives were going to be hell—my dad included. My God, I was a silent tyrant. I iced my staff with sharp looks, sighs of disappointment, walking off in the middle of conversations, and open brooding. The office walked on eggshells. No matter how you sliced it, the situation was ugly.

As one might expect, that discontent followed me into my home like a stray puppy. The guy that once came home energized, helped around the house, and did chores with joy turned into a sad sulker obsessed with money and saving face. I became distant. The voice had become a constant companion, and in order to solve my problems, I needed room to think, quiet time. Slowly but surely, I started to isolate and live inside my own head. I was in pain and didn't know what to do; nothing in my life eased the suffering for more than a fleeting moment.

Then one day, a day so beautifully sunny that one would wish every day could be the same, I walked off my boat and heard laughter. Rewind for a moment, to the story of my first drink. Do you remember my parents' party? Keep it in the back of your mind as you read on.

I heard the laughter and thought, *Wow, those people are happy. I wish I felt like that.* It was a group of those friends whom I secretly envied, and they were enjoying themselves after a day on the water. I meandered over and joined them. What jumped out immediately was the ruddy glow of alcohol on their cheeks; it seemed almost angelic. At that point, I hadn't had a drink in five years. And I had never shielded myself from environments where people drank because I was never tempted. Well, things had changed. It wasn't that I wanted a drink, per se; I only wanted to feel better. I said sheepishly, "I'll take one of those Mike's Hard Lemonades," and I thought, *It's a girly drink, for crying out loud. Nothing's going to happen.*

CHAPTER 28

A single Mike's Hard Lemonade isn't going to get anybody drunk. I'm not sure of the alcohol content, but it couldn't have been very much. Plus, I was careful: I took my time, tiptoeing into an area I'd never been able manage in the past. I was testing myself, and I passed with flying colors. I was able to have just one. On the way back to my boat, I thought, *You know, Charlie, if you really tried, you could use alcohol responsibly. Look at what just happened. It was easy, for crying out loud. You could do that all day and never have a problem.*

Wait, did you hear that? The collective scream of my brothers in sobriety from across the globe? They just yelled, "No, you can't!" And they're correct.

You know the Kraken, right? If not, let me give you a quick profile. He's a legendary sea monster, and if there's even a hint he might get loose, Zeus gets nervous and calls an emergency meeting of the gods. That's right—the Kraken is such a badass that almighty Zeus calls in help. Well, drinking that bottle of Mike's was like unlocking the Kraken's cage. True, it didn't get me drunk, but it did something much worse: it gave me an ever so slight sense of ease, a false hope—more fool's gold. And here's what happened: I foolishly thought all I needed was to drink a little more, just the right amount, and everything would be fine. My mind began to spin with that idea. I can't say I completely disregarded the historical data of me and booze, but I certainly rewrote the past in less harsh terms—revisionist history. I was much stronger and in control, and alcohol wasn't quite as domineering. When I finished telling myself lies, I anxiously looked forward to the next weekend at the marina.

I have an illness of body and mind. When substance enters my body, regardless of the brand or amount, triggers go off. My mind can't stop thinking about what my body craves, and my body craves what my mind can't stop thinking about. It creates a super-turbo, hurricane effect as thoughts feed off each other and grow stronger. I locked on like a pit bull. I was already thinking about the next bottle of Mike's before I laid down for the night.

The idea arrested my thoughts during the week, too. When the stress of being a small business owner hit, I'd think about the weekend. Not about the day on the water with my wife and kids; I skipped right over that part. I envisioned the moment I would slip into the circle and ask, "Hey, you have another one of those Mike's?" I imagined the cold bottle on my lips and ultimately a giant sigh of relief as I escaped my troubles.

The weekend came soon enough, and all went according to plan. Typically we went to the boat on Friday and stayed the weekend. On Sunday evening Molly would take the girls home so that they could get ready for school, leaving me alone on the boat. The store was closed on Mondays, so I'd usually go out with my dad, and he'd drop me off at home afterward. I had a window between the time Molly left and my dad arrived, and that was when I would make my move.

We spent Sunday on the water, as was our custom. When I noticed my friends as I docked, my heartbeat quickened. Soon enough, I kissed my wife good-bye and watched her leave. I don't recall whether or not I cleaned up; if I did, it was the bare minimum. Then I hurried to join the festivities. Remember, until the weekend before, I hadn't had a drink in five years; none of my new friends had ever seen me drink. With that in mind, how might you explain that as soon as I joined the circle, someone asked, "Hey, Charlie! You want a Mike's?"

The power of intention.

We are so much more powerful than we know or believe. The truth is that we attract to our lives those things we think about. Call it hocus-pocus if you will, but it's true. If you want good things in your life, then think good thoughts and brace yourself for your biggest dream to slowly manifest. Obviously, it works in reverse as well.

I drank the Mike's a tad faster than I had the week before, and with a little more purpose. But instead of going home, I hunkered down and had a second one. I needed just one more to fully lubricate my stress.

If a single hard lemonade unlocked the Kraken's cage, well, number two was like walking inside and kicking him in face. It was the perfect amount needed to jumpstart rusty pathways in my brain. Just that quickly, in a moment of time equal to a lightning flash, I was back in my old mindset. The animal that lived inside of me roared, *Feed me!*

I need a real drink, I thought. *Not this sissy, sweet, foo-foo crap. I want rum or bourbon or vodka—a man's drink, straight with no chaser.*

I'd already pushed the limit with my friends, though. I certainly couldn't ask them; they might think I was trying to do what I was trying to do: catch a buzz. And the way those people gossiped, it would get back to Molly in a heartbeat, which was the last thing I needed. I eased my way out of the circle and vanished.

I imagine someone looked up and asked, "Hey, where's Charlie?"

Charlie was belly-up at the bar, that's where Charlie was.

I hopped a taxi over to the next town and found the local watering hole. I slammed vodka like it was a rattlesnake antidote and I'd been bitten. I sat there until last call, knocking back all I could get my hands on until I was absolutely hammered.

I woke up the next morning on my boat, pasty mouthed, queasy, and with a sledgehammer of a headache. The details about how I got there were as foggy as the tail end of the night melds into something similar to a dreamscape. Bits and pieces sat on the horizon but dissipated as soon I got close. I didn't go home to Molly, though—I was drunk, not crazy.

I pulled myself together as best as I could because this wasn't a typical Monday. The girls didn't have school, and Molly was coming down with some of her friends. I needed to practice my act. I worked out a quick story about eating some bad shellfish and falling asleep. I went over my lines a couple of times until they came out naturally. I put on my sunglasses and waited.

Here's the thing about those of us who suffer from addiction. We don't want to use; we know that it's a dead end and that checking out into an altered mind state never solves the problem. As hard as you might try, you can't stay inebriated forever; I know this from personal experience. Eventually, you have to come down. And when you do, all the misery you were trying to drink or smoke away has quadrupled.

All I'd set out to do was ease a little stress, but now not only did I have the anxiety I'd started with, I also had a heavy dose of post-drunk guilt. I felt horrible. I kept seeing the pain in Molly's eyes when she found out what I'd done, and I couldn't let that happen.

CHAPTER 29

Picture perusing the fruit and vegetable section of your local grocery store when a basket of strawberries catches your eye. The fruit is the most beautiful you've ever seen, red and plump. You're enticed by their appearance and make the purchase, and boy, are you glad you did. Upon first bite, the sweetly tart juice explodes on your palate and drips down your fingers; those strawberries are lip-smacking good, quite possibly the tastiest you've ever had. You smile, kick up your feet, and savor the entire basket.

Then a half hour later, your throat begins to swell and your breathing becomes labored. Your skin erupts in hives, and you itch all over. At this point you might say to yourself, *Hmm, I must be allergic to strawberries.* That would be a logical assumption, right?

Next time in the store, you see a basket that looks even better than the last one: bigger and plumper with a promising color of deep, dark red. A logical mind wouldn't touch that basket with a ten-foot pole. Right? Because by then you would have deduced how you felt pre-strawberries and the struggle to breathe after consumption. You wouldn't need a doctor's test with an explanation of the results. It would be easier to simply cut out strawberries. When it comes to breathing, why take the risk?

I often use the strawberry story when I speak because it paints a vivid picture of the true depth of my sickness. I'll say, "If alcohol were berries, I kept going back and buying basket after basket. And I did it in spite of overwhelming evidence that I was allergic."

Let's pause and chew on that behavior for a second. I *knew* alcohol was bad for me. Our history together included destruction of colossal proportions—a near-death experience, even. Nevertheless, I was about to test the waters yet again. How does one explain such a thing? It doesn't make logical sense. What I eventually came to realize was that my illness didn't reside in the realm of logic. My illness was of the spiritual variety.

Spiritual sickness is the only explanation for addiction that seems to make any sense. We substance addicts, when disconnected from the divine, mistakenly chase after fleeting moments of peace through alcohol or drugs. It doesn't matter that our throats might swell, our skin might itch, or our breathing becomes troubled. We simply want that moment, that slice of time when everything is perfect and the pain is gone. And we will chase it to the ends of the Earth, until our dying breath. You've passed by us before on the street: tattered, disheveled, stinky, asking if you might spare a quarter. Next time, instead of rushing past and wondering why we can't get our act together, offer a silent blessing for our healing. Pray for us, for a miracle, for an awakening that will allow us to somehow see our true God.

I realize you might find my idea as a simple answer to a complex problem. But as far as I can see, that *has* to be the answer, at least for me. Logic would suggest my crash and tumble off the wagon following the Mike's would raise a few red flags. *Warning, Charlie, danger ahead!* Clearly booze and Charlie didn't mix. I guess one might say I was on a quest to meet my higher power, traveling that rocky road to see how bad I really wanted know him: my God. Not the one who was given to me at Mass, neatly packaged like a Happy Meal; that guy wasn't going to get the job done. His back wasn't strong enough, and the lifting was about to get real heavy.

Honestly, that night at the bar scared me big time. It rang as a clear reminder of what could happen to my life if I wasn't careful. I didn't run out and tie one on the next weekend. In fact, it was about three months before I took another drink.

Three months of bricks stacking on my shoulders. Three months of that corset tightening on my chest. Three months icing my staff about slumping sales. Three months of envying those doing better than me. And finally I had to feel better. So I drank, and it was so very good, like catching up with a dear friend I hadn't seen in years. We picked up right where we'd left off, and I was very careful and didn't overdo it. This was my cycle for a while: three months of escalating stress followed by a couple of "responsible" drinks. I thought of vodka like migraines sufferers might think of prescription medication: I'd only go to the strong stuff when the pain became unbearable and over-the-counter pills didn't work.

Soon, however, the space between drinks began to close. Every three months turned into every other month. That soon became once a month, and eventually I was drinking regularly. And nobody suspected a thing. I did such a good job of hiding it, of never going overboard, that it was never a thought in anyone's mind that I might be drinking. I mistakenly believed I had mastered the art of responsible alcohol consumption.

There came a time when Molly was out of town with the girls. I don't recall exactly where she went, but I do remember she would be gone for about four days. Saturday rolled around, and it had been a particularly brutal work week, one of those that makes a small business owner sigh and think, *Why am I even doing this? There's gotta be an easier way to earn a buck.* I decided to hit the bar, open up the pressure valve, and let off some steam. My plan was to have a couple of pops and then come back home. I got dressed and topped it off with my wicked Ducati jacket. Then I hopped on my scooter and hit the town. Guided by fate, I landed in one of the spots I'd frequented back in the day. I grabbed a seat at the bar and ordered what I thought would be the first of two drinks.

My history with addiction is that of a binger, by the way. As you may have noticed, I go long periods without a single thought of using drugs or alcohol, but then something happens. It's as if the solar system aligns just right, I get the signal, and I shift into high gear. This turned out to be one of those nights. Before I knew it, one drink had turned into four. I was at the bar having the time of my life. I'm that guy—you know, the one holding court, storytelling and buying all my new best friends drinks, laughing, and feeling no pain.

I've often wondered why the thought I'm about to share came to the forefront of my mind. It was an idea I acted on that ended up taking my family and me on a journey of indescribable pain and suffering. On some level, I know it was the vodka. There still lived in me a thrill seeker that seemed to ignite with the addition of alcohol. I could just as easily have hopped on my souped-up scooter and blasted down the road full throttle, however I didn't choose that. Again, I've often wondered why. The question inevitably has no answer, and I am reminded that life is perfect. I surrender to the idea that I had to walk the primrose path to find my God. And truth be told, I believe it was so that I could tell you this story.

So what was the thought?

As the bartender brought my fourth vodka, I thought, *A little nose candy would be nice right about now...*

Chapter 30

Brace yourself. You're about to read two words that could very well cause you to gasp in horror, choke on your latte, or drop the wineglass. You might even slap your leg and exclaim, "Oh no, Charlie!" startling the passenger seated next to you on your flight. You can't say I didn't warn you, though. Well, here they are.

Crack cocaine.

For most Americans, those words conjure thoughts of seedy, dimly lit, urban street corners. Teens with baggy pants and hoodies. Wandering, emaciated crackheads, virtual zombies willing to do anything for just one more hit. You've seen the images in theaters and television, right? *The Wire,* one of HBO's big hits, received rave reviews for its realistic portrayal of a budding crack empire in Baltimore. The Wiki description even describes it as *"Appearing primarily in impoverished inner-city neighborhoods in New York, Los Angeles, and Miami in late 1984 and 1985."*

Well, a few years later crack cocaine had made it all the way to wholesome Waterbury, Connecticut, population one hundred thousand, and we met each other that night at the bar. It was an instant love affair.

Before I give you details of how it took me to hell, I'd like to rewind for a moment. I promised early on that my story wouldn't be a salacious retelling of drug use. There are hundreds of places to find that stuff, if that's what you seek. I'm not going there. Besides, I can't imagine that given our endless obsession with suffering, you haven't witnessed a soul being slow-burned by drug use. Do you really need to read that worn-out story again?

I offer this instead.

Close your eyes for a moment and think of the person you love most in the universe. Inside your loved one is a loneliness that is as black as tar and as thick as crude oil—pain so viscid their heart struggles to pump. And you can see it. The sadness in their eyes is obvious no matter how hard they try to hide it. Underneath the forced smiles and on-call happy is deep sorrow that you don't understand; sadness is a foreign emotion in your world. So when you ask, *How are you? Is everything okay?* "I'm fine. Great! Couldn't be any better," are lies that twist in your gut like a dagger.

You're helpless with hands tied behind your back, and you're forced to spectate as they take a hammer and chisel away the good pieces of their soul, as a sculpture does to stone. Each blow causes them to silently wince, and yet they keep hammering. Terrified, you come to realize what being sculpted is black like death—their own death. Sure as the day is long, it is a march toward certain death. The worst part is that there's nothing you can do. Unless a miracle happens, this person you love deeply is going to die.

When you think of drug abuse in those terms, it leaves you with only one thought: "How do we fix it?" Suddenly it no longer matters how someone ended up on the path of destruction; all that matters is getting it corrected as soon as possible and by any means necessary. You gain a fine focus and look for help from wherever and whomever. I've seen even the casual believer raise eyes toward the heavens and say, "God, help me, please."

That's what this story is about. Ultimately, it's about help. Acknowledge the problem, of course. But don't linger too long, because we're marching toward a solution, a fix that worked for me and that I believe will work for you. It doesn't matter that your Kraken may be present in overeating, obsessive shopping, gambling, or whatever; everybody has something. The truth is that when you want change bad enough, when you have a burning desire to get well and nothing else matters, then it can happen. I'm living proof that who you were doesn't have to be who you are. I'm about to tell you how far I fell—so far there was no other earthly place for me to go. The next step was death. That's nothing to glorify, I'll remind you. I don't consider it a badge of honor; in fact if I could have raised my hand and said, "Hello, I'm Charlie Collins, and I can tell you how to overcome challenges," bypassing the airing of my dirty laundry, I would have. But this had to be a peer-to-peer narrative, if for nothing else that for credibility. Now, let us move on.

I jokingly tell my audiences, "That night at the bar was the night I met my higher power." I can laugh about it today because now I understand from where the Kraken derives his power. A roar that for five years shook me to the core now falls on my ears like the purr of a kitten.

My pain was thick and black. I didn't have any coping mechanisms; I wasn't going to meetings. I was the ideal crack customer. If a corporation had conducted a market survey or focus group, I'm certain they would have concluded with a description of me: a risk taker with low self-esteem, disposable income, and an addictive personality. In me, the character of cocaine in freebase form found a brain that was craving escapism. It was a match made in hell. What follows is my best attempt to explain how this drug took over my life.

Cocaine interferes with a chemical messenger in the brain called dopamine. Dopamine is involved in pleasure response, released by cells during activities like eating or having sex. Under normal conditions it gets released and then quickly reabsorbed. A person feels really good for a bit, and then it's back to normal. Well, crack interrupts the cycle; it screws with dopamine's normal reabsorption process, so dopamine builds up, creating a lingering feeling of exhilaration or euphoria.

Let's quickly go back one more time before moving on. If you recall, we started this journey with me talking about some of my earliest memories. I've been honest and openly shared my fears, hopes, and dreams, so I think you know me pretty well at this point. What do you think happened after I took the first hit?

I was a duck who'd been living in the Mojave Desert and suddenly discovered there were ten thousand lakes in Minnesota. It was *exactly* what I had been looking for, and I was hooked in a nanosecond. My brain said, *Crack, where have you been my whole life?* I had never experienced anything close to it. Time stopped, and I existed in a state of total peace; that's really what I thought. I just knew I had found the answer to all of my problems.

Obviously, I had no idea of the widespread destruction that would follow; I was only trying to ease my pain. Every component of my personal and professional lives would be turned upside down and shaken, their composition repeatedly tested.

But the seed was planted, and my illness of body and mind kicked into overdrive. I had the idea that I could slip away into ease and comfort with just a hit of crack. I could feel better than I ever had, instantly erase a lifetime of pain. All I had to do was fire up.

About three weeks later, I had thoroughly convinced myself it was the right thing to do, and I tried it for the second time. The addiction happened quickly after that. In my typical pattern three weeks' lag time became once every two weeks. Every other week quickly became once a week. Within three months, I was using daily, escaping every time the opportunity presented itself.

I remember the eleven months that followed like raindrops blur a camera lens. Along the way I felt myself sinking, and I had this eerie feeling of déjà vu. *This feels like Willows all over again,* I would occasionally think. However, I told myself I could stop whenever I wanted. It was maybe the nine-month mark when I began to seriously tell myself it was time to stop. It had become nearly impossible to keep up the double life. I had been hiding my use from Molly—or at least I thought I was. I mean, how much work really needed to be done at the office at midnight? She was no fool, and I knew that she suspected something was not quite right. Not only was I returning to the office to "work" almost nightly, but my eating habits were whacked out, I was losing weight, and I wasn't sleeping. One day she said, "You need to see the doctor and get your thyroid checked out."

I knew the true reasons for my physical decline but still went to the doctor for the test. "My thyroid's fine," I announced. "See? There's nothing wrong. Just a little stress."

By month twelve, I knew I had a very serious problem. I won't lie and say I wanted to stop at that point, because I enjoyed getting high; it made me feel good. What I wanted, however, was to be in control, and it had become clear that I had zero ability to supervise the Kraken. He had taken over, and it seemed my priorities had become about responding to his roaring. I tried a set of rules. *I won't use at work. Never at work. I'll spend time with my wife and kids first. If I do use at all, I'll do it after they go to bed.* And I meant it. Every word.

But it was impossible to stick to the plan. The cravings for ease and comfort became too strong and dominated my life.

Domination is a relative term, so let me add some metrics. Move the problem out of the esoteric realm and into cold, hard financial facts. Early on, the habit cost me about $300 bucks per week to feed. At its height, when the Kraken was roaring uncontrollably, it was easily four times that amount per week. With no one keeping an eye on me, slowly I drained our life savings. I wrote myself checks from Vision Dynamics accounts. I took cash advances off my credit cards. I dug a financial hole that would take years to fill.

I don't think it's possible to adequately explain the level of guilt that began to torment me. Remember, this wasn't my first rodeo. I was repeating a familiar cycle and constantly beat myself up about being such an idiot. But I couldn't control it.

Molly began to question me. "Why do you need to go to the office tonight? Why aren't you ever around? The girls miss their father. What's going on, Charlie? Something's wrong—I can feel it!" Her pain was right there in front of me, in her voice and in her eyes. And she was right about my daughters: they absolutely adored me. If it was up to them, they would have ridden on my kneecaps every waking moment. And I would have loved nothing better. But the Kraken that had been born inside of me was stronger. I slowly withdrew from my family.

The sheer addictiveness of crack cocaine is hard to imagine if you've never been there. It is a cruel master that works on its victims psychologically and physiologically. In addition to being a pacifier, it causes the brain to produce less dopamine. And that's why I was using it in the first place—so that I could feel good! But now, what used to get me high wasn't enough. I had to increase the amount in order to reach my place of ease and comfort. It's kind of like the heavy sodium content in cola drinks that cause people to crave more cola drinks. Ultimately I got to the point where I had a hard time functioning without it.

But I couldn't keep up the double life. My world was falling apart at the seams. I decided to come clean and tell my wife everything.

CHAPTER 31

Remember the recovery process I described after electrocuting myself on the train? Remember how I talked of it being the most excruciating pain one could ever imagine—bathing my open wounds in saltwater, taking a straight razor to pare away dead flesh? It was brutal and not something I'd wish upon anyone. I'm going to use that experience to get you in ballpark of what my path of recovery was like for my wife. But before I do that, I want to share something.

Molly loves me. I mean, she *really* loves me. And it's not that "as long as she feels good" kind of love. It's deep and wide and true and sturdy enough to hold me up when I couldn't do it for myself. This isn't speculation or guesswork on my part, either; I've seen it manifested in action.

Marriage comes with a built-in set of complications; that's simply part of the deal. The vows you utter before the world are going to get tested. As it turns out, for many it's *just talk,* words they say as a part of a larger ceremony. I don't need to quote statistics on divorce, because you already know what I'm talking about.

For my wife, her vows weren't just talk, and thank God. When she said "for better and for worse," it meant something; it was a real commitment of love and devotion. She stood by my side, unwavering, through the absolute worst of the worst. Even when my mother suggested she take the kids and move on, Molly fought her. When I became a mere shadow of the man she'd married, she held on and believed I would get better. How she knew, I have yet to figure that out. All that's clear is I would have never made it without her.

Think of my drug use as causing her full-body, third-degree burns that require salt baths, straight razor skin peeling, and extensive physical therapy. But she's a gamer; she grits her teeth and comes out the other side ready to move on. No sooner than she recovers, however, I flambé her again. And again and again. Remember, it took eight trips to rehab, costing us a bundle, before I truly stepped on the path to recovery. I don't think it takes a PhD to figure out life for my family was horrid.

After the initial confession, I tell my audiences, "I went on an extensive journey of R and R." Everyone smiles and exhales, thinking, *Okay he's finally getting it together.* I can feel the tension come back when I say, "It wasn't rest and relaxation—it was rehab and relapse."

I wasn't nearly ready to stop using. The honest answer is I went to rehab the first few times just to get people off my back. Eventually my parents were in the circle of knowledge. Like Molly, they couldn't grasp why on earth I would turn to drugs again, after all I'd been through. They were slack-jawed, confused, and baffled. And of all things, crack cocaine? "My goodness, Charlie," my mom said as she shook her head. "That's heavy-duty drugs. What's the matter with you? Nobody in their right mind would touch that stuff."

I guess you could say a mother knows best: I wasn't close to being in a healthy state of mind. And quite honestly, the drugs made me feel good, better than ever before, and that's what I needed. The cycle of mounting anxiety, followed by a binge, followed by massive guilt was on repeat, skipping like a scratched record. It was like being stuck in a maze of doors. It didn't matter which one I opened; I got more of the same: the pressure to be present, to be engaged, to be a husband and father and business owner was relentless. Ever pressing, ever demanding. But so was my need to escape to that place where it didn't matter if I was perfect. I needed to float away into ease and comfort. And believe it or not, there was still a part of me that was determined to control the cravings.

Sadly, rehab became a place where I simply went. I wasn't there to get better—I didn't even try. I used it to rest up after burning both ends of the candle to nubs. It gave me a chance to detox, get plenty of sleep, and eat decent food. Those early trips were never about truly looking for the source of my addiction. I'd go through the motions at the required meetings, the whole time thinking, *I'm nothing like these people. They have no idea what it's like to suffer like me. I'm legally blind.* That self-talk sounds familiar, like childhood Charlie, doesn't it?

I'd personally changed lives by showing people they really didn't see with their eyes; I had stacks of letters from customers telling me as much. I'd preached, "You can be whole, live a full life—legal blindness doesn't matter!" And it worked, and they bought products from me.

However, the very deepest part of me still had not accepted my own situation. I would *never* become like my hero, Magnum PI; I would *never* jump out of planes or drive a racecar. Consequently, my self-talk was self-destructive. *My eyes are bad, and I'm less than. My pain is greater than anyone can ever know. It doesn't matter what I do; I'm a loser and will never amount to much.* One more time I'll state the obvious here: that's all bad. Love must start with the person in the mirror, and the fastest way to get started is to look yourself in the eye and say, "Everything is perfect in this moment. I'm right where I need to be." Then give yourself a smile and hug and get on with your life. If ever you feel yourself slipping, find a mirror and repeat it as many times as needed. Again, who you are has nothing to do with who you become. One of the tenets of yoga that I love is the belief that each breath is a new beginning. I know this to be truth today, but back then, I was clueless.

I'd come home from rehab refreshed, a few pounds heavier, and full of promises. "I'll never do it again. That was my last trip to rehab. You can take that to the bank."

At most I'd last a couple of months before I was back at it with a vengeance. It seemed after each stint in rehab, the Kraken only got stronger.

CHAPTER 32

When I was hooked on crack, my life began to unravel at an alarming pace. Every component took a downward trajectory, physical health and spiritual health. My financial health, once the fuel of my happiness, suffered a double whammy of crippling force. On the one hand, Vision Dynamics was a rudderless ship. I'd show up from time to time, but I wasn't present. I was a shell of the man that had launched the company. At one juncture I had more than 3,200 emails in my box. I wasn't returning phone calls, either. And let's not forget, I was the face of Vision Dynamics, its chief marketer, the idea guy. It was my personal story that brought people to the store. But now I was MIA and strung out, and competition was increasing. I'm sure you can imagine what happened to our sales numbers.

That's just the one hand. On the other one, the company was feeding my insanely expensive habit plus the subsequent trips to rehab. Early on, nobody noticed I was sucking money out of the company; they didn't have cause to think I would do anything other than what was right. At some point along the way, Molly looked at the books and realized I'd brought Vision Dynamics to the point of financial ruin. That's when I experienced one of her multifaceted forms of love—the tough kind. She stood up, said enough, and took legal action to remove me as a signor.

While I was demolishing the foundation of my family's financial health, I was doing even worse to the fabric that tied us together. I could not be trusted. It's painful to admit even after all these years. You see, I was raised by a man who instilled the idea that someone's word and handshake is better than a written contract. That credo is one of my guiding principles today; I won't do business with people I can't trust. However, under the stupor of substance, my word was worthless. When it came to the Kraken, it didn't matter what I *might* have said. When he roared, everything else was canceled, and I went off to get high.

My life went on like this for a few years: a roller coaster of binging and rehab, brief periods of iron-willed sobriety, followed by a tumble, then repeat. The highs were never quite as good as the time before, and the lows grew deeper and darker. Eventually it got to the point where smoking crack wasn't working anymore. Instead of bringing ease and comfort, I could feel it driving me closer to all-out mental collapse. The psychosis that comes with prolonged drug use showed up: agitation, paranoia, delusions, thoughts of violence, and guess who else? My old friend, suicide.

Let's glance at the variables in my life: me, my family, my business, and all the limbs that branch from those trees. There was nothing good. At this point, my wife was ready to leave, my business was failing, and I was slowly marching toward ending it all. Life couldn't get any worse. But here's something interesting: even in the midst of all the blackness, my moral compass never stopped pinging. It was a distant ring, but nevertheless I sometimes heard it. In those moments when I did, I'd look my wife in the eye and promise I would never do it again. Herein lies the greatest testament of Molly's love: she heard me. Our family was going up in flames, and by all rights she should have bailed, but she didn't. The moral of the story is to never give up because there's always hope.

At the time, however, I couldn't see a way out. I decided it was time to end the pain. I concluded there was no way that I could keep up the life I was living; I couldn't control myself. The havoc I was reaping on my wife and kids, and anyone else who got close, was too much. The guilt associated with my hurting others was ten tons, and I couldn't carry it another second. At least when I died, something good would come of it: Molly would get insurance money and go on to find a man that she deserved. My kids were young enough that at most I'd be a blip in their memory.

I'd heard of people having heart attacks from cocaine overdose, so that was my plan: I'd smoke myself to death. I don't quite recall the amount of crack I purchased, but it was more than enough to do the job. I checked into a hotel room and gave explicit instructions that I was not to be disturbed. "I'm on a very important business assignment," I said. "It's imperative that my whereabouts remain confidential."

I began to smoke. And smoke. And smoke. Wanting to die.

I kept smoking until there was no more. All that came of that night was intensified, paranoid, tweaking. I barricaded myself in the bathroom; my mind buzzing like it was filled with a hive of bumblebees.

In the opening you may recall I said, "It takes a certain amount of audacity to believe one's life story could benefit someone else." I really believe that. But after all the years of reckless living, exhibiting a silent death wish, and then finally going for it and coming up short, what else was I to conclude? My life has to be about sharing my journey so that others might find hope.

CHAPTER 33

Shortly after I came up short in the hotel bathroom, my anger with God soared to an all-time high. I honestly hadn't thought about him much during my cycle of relapse and rehab, but now he was on my mind. I thought, *Okay let me get this straight. You take my eyes away. You leave me in the most unbearable pain one can imagine. And when I try to kill myself, you won't let me go? What the hell?* I was sick and tired of the pain and had finally reached my breaking point.

Let's start with the moment that I realized I was different, the instant that I knew something was wrong. I've suggested that perhaps it began those first few days, with my struggle to breathe. Now let's fast-forward through my life, collecting moments I've described in this narrative. I realize that it's impossible to capture all that makes up my psyche, however you know enough to see that the theme of my life was fatalistic. Let's say we collect self-pity, fear, disappointment, shame, the many faces of anger, and the negative self-talk, and we put them in a container. It's a lifetime's worth, so were talking commercial trash dumpster size.

Now, let's place me naked in the center of a parking lot. I want you to maneuver the dumpster high above my head and then turn it upside down and let all that poison spill on my crown. Watch as the weight of my life, all at once, crushes me to ground and buries me. Shake out the last drop, please.

That was an attempt to illustrate the night I finally surrendered under the weight of my life. You've witnessed the scene in movies: the character looks at himself in the mirror and finally sees the truth; the reality of what he's *really* become causes him to spin into a tornado of emotion. The first move shatters the mirror with a fist—an attempt to punch the monster they see right in the chops. The glass cuts a bloody gash, but he doesn't miss a stroke. Furniture gets heaved, tables are stomped and splintered into toothpicks, holes are punched in the walls. While this happens, the character emits a sound that doesn't sound human; it's an animalistic waling that comes from a broken soul, an anguish so deep that one doesn't even recognize its tone. Finally, after the raw emotion has burned off like gas, the character falls to his knees in a pile of debris, weeping. "God, if you are real," he cries to the heavens, "I need to know. I mean, I could really use some help here. I can't keep going like this."

That was the scene that played out in my basement the night I surrendered.

After the hotel episode I went home and slunk through the door with my tail tucked deeply between my legs. All alone, (Molly was at work) the level of remorse, guilt and shame, climbed to a level that is beyond words. I was defeated. My soul ached. I'd often thought of death as a way to end the pain. And finally, when the suffering had gotten so bad that I'd decided to do something about it, I failed. *You've got to be kidding me*, I thought. *You can't even get that right, Charlie...* I spent the day in darkness, my mind abuzz with the chatter of a lifetime of failure. I cursed mightily at God! I didn't understand how he could be so cruel. This last move took the cake. He'd created me inferior making certain I would never amount to anything. That was bad enough. But, in his most merciless act of all, he wouldn't let me die? And so I spun out of control, destroying my basement and eventually landing in a place of total surrender.

The Kraken was too much for me to handle alone. I was Zeus calling for help. I committed, in that moment. *I will do whatever it takes to end the pain.* Just that quick, in the twinkling of an eye, my life changed. I stepped on the path to recovery fully committed to doing the work—and believe me, it was the biggest battle of my life.

CHAPTER 34

I entered rehab for the eighth time and finally met my God—a God that Charlie Collins could call his very own. Upon introduction, the bricks on my shoulders fell away, the corset loosened around my chest, and I took a full, refreshing breath. The buzzing hive of ego-driven thoughts slowed; the companion voice of negativity began to lose its clout. Although the Kraken still roared, he was banished to his cage. All of this happened by *truly* embracing the principles in the *Big Book of Alcoholics Anonymous.* The God I met—or in the vernacular of AA, "the power greater than myself"—was nothing like the gods I'd worshipped before. It wasn't at all like the God of my Catholic youth, who kept a punitive eye on me. It was not even close to the god I found in the vodka bottle who told me lies. He was far from my twin gods of money and prestige, who were really holograms. He certainly wasn't that devil in a god costume, crack cocaine. He was compassionate, understanding, long-suffering, loving, and most of all forgiving. As silly as it may sound, he allowed me to finally be human. It was with an understanding that I didn't have to be perfect that I moved into my sobriety.

Unbeknownst to me, I had taken the first of the twelve steps that night in my basement: I genuinely admitted that I was powerless over alcohol and drugs. The operative word is *genuine.* I'd said it before but never really meant it. Powerless? Charlie "Padre" Collins? You're kidding me! I believed that I could will my way to accomplish whatever I wanted. And I had evidence. I'd survived electrocution. The doctors wanted to cut my arm off. They dumped me in salt baths... You know the story.

Not only did I live, but I thrived, and I did it all with my mind. But this substance battle was one I could not win with will. Clearly it was a different kind of fight, with rules I didn't yet understand. It had nothing to do with strength; in fact, I would learn it was just the opposite. It was about surrender, about giving in, about admitting, "I'm powerless in this fight, and I need help." And so I did.

I find it amazing, what we are able to see once we become aware. Things we missed that were right before our eyes seem to magically appear. You've had the experience, right? What happens after you buy a new car? You suddenly see your model all over town. They were there the whole time, but you never noticed. Well, that's what the rehab experience was like for me on try number eight.

First of all, hearing and *accepting* the truth that I had a sickness was profound. I mean, what a way to kick-start my journey into sobriety. It gave me a framework, a container in which to place my past behavior and make sense of it. It meant that I wasn't a bad person hell-bent on destroying myself and my family. This revelation put me in the game. It suggested I could be an active participant in my sobriety by taking steps to get well. Furthermore, it made my choices so plain and simple that I wondered why I hadn't figured it out on my own.

- Choice A: If I drink, I get what I've gotten: pain and misery. Confirmed. No ambiguity there.
- Choice B: Don't drink, and live a life free of pain and misery. And who knows what could happen? Infinite possibilities!

Obviously I'd heard all the *Big Book* rhetoric before; it went in one ear and right out the other. Just like my unwillingness to embrace juvenile macular degeneration, I hadn't been ready to accept that I was sick with alcoholism. But this time I didn't ignore the overwhelming evidence. I stood tall in that first meeting in rehab and said, "Hi, my name is Charlie, and I'm an alcoholic." I meant every word.

Although I didn't realize it at the time, the ignition that would lead me to be a motivational speaker and write this book was turned on during my eighth trip to rehab. While sitting in the meetings—this time without judgment and actually embracing the material—I found that others were just like me. I suddenly realized that no matter what a person looked like on the outside, inside the suffering was identical. True, their torment and fear weren't driven by a childhood revelation of blindness; I still had a lock on that crown. But pain is pain is pain. I finally heard the stories of abuse and abandonment, of suffering wrapped in a different package than mine but suffering nevertheless. I was moved with indescribable empathy and compassion. The calling that had been unearthed while recovering from my burns woke up. But first things first: I had to get well.

You've taken the journey through my life thus far and have a good idea of how I approach the things I want. So, what do you think happened next? I slammed the pedal to the floor and went after my sobriety full-speed ahead. I committed to the twelve-step program, and I left rehab a new person. On the inside, where it most counted, I was brand-new. My family wasn't so convinced I would make it, and rightfully so, but I knew I would. I never had a doubt because I was willing to do whatever it took to stay sober.

In addition to fully embracing all things AA (going to meetings, finding a sponsor, working the twelve steps, and walking the talk), I began to devour books like a madman. True to form, I went on a mission of information gathering. Just like I approached engines, I figured that if I knew how I ticked, I could make myself better. I started with titles focusing on the brain and decision-making. I wanted to know why, given all the information available, I had made such bad choices. Very early on a whole new world opened up to me. With this knowledge in hand, I created a personal sobriety plan that worked like a charm.

Before I share the broad strokes of what worked for me, let me be clear: I am not a certified doctor or scientist. What I am, however, is someone who was deathly ill. And in order to be an active player in my healing, I've read lots of material (over two hundred books and at least a thousand articles) about how to get well. I've taken that information, conducted experiments on myself, and had positive results. Follow close as I share a sample of my work; I believe the principles are universal.

The logic, or hypothesis if you will, behind my initial work stems from the concept that our brains are essentially programmable computers. I assumed that if over the years I had unknowingly programmed myself to react in fear and turn to substance on impulse, then conversely I should be able to program myself to do something different. Makes sense, right? I mapped out a strategy that in many ways mirrored a military attack plan. I broke down the components of my habits step by step, and I created a plan to disrupt the cycle while I developed healthy routines.

Think about it like this: When addicts use, we exist in a world of triggers, involuntary impulses, and knee-jerk behaviors that are filled with coconspirators. It's not like we can see the traps coming, either; they spring on us like sinkholes when we are least prepared. Over time these subtle yet complex ways of being create deep, interconnected pathways in our brain. I quickly realized it would be impossible to undo thirty-plus years' worth of that harm, so my plan was about creating new pathways in my brain—a new complexity of healthy associations and habits.

My number-one target was stress. It was easy to calculate that my inability to properly manage anxiety, regardless of the stimulus, would lead me to drink. Stress mounts, and I reach for vodka; once I have the first drink, everyone knows where that leads. If I was going to survive, it was mandatory that I manage stress.

Two of the first things I did was change my diet and shut off the television.

I won't dive into the relationship between food and our mental well-being; a simple Google search will give you a plethora of information on the subject. What I will tell you, however, is that sugar and salt are addictive. Addiction is addiction, in my eyes, so I cut out fast food and that late-night bowl of ice cream I so dearly loved. I went through the cabinets on a rampage, tossing processed food items that had been our staples. Molly will tell you I went overboard, but she'll say it with a smile of course.

I don't think anyone would disagree that the news can be a downer. For reasons that would require another book to explain, television news peddles 99 percent fear—asteroids and swine flu and gun control and recession and politics and war and threats of war. After the news, what remains isn't much better. Therefore it was off with the tube.

The next thing I did was program an hourly reminder on every computer I owned. Every sixty minutes, I got a message: "Stop, Relax, Breathe, Think, Act." I wrote it on Post-It notes and plastered them throughout the house. Everywhere I went there was a reminder to breathe easy.

I book-ended my days with reflection before bed and meditation upon waking. The nightly reflection was an insurance policy against going to sleep with angst. I couldn't afford to have subconscious weeds of anxiety sprouting in corners I couldn't see, so I would spend an hour evaluating my day and taking inventory of how well I served. One of the concepts that surfaced during rehab was a need to give. I'd lived my entire life on a quest to see how much I could get for Charlie. My new credo was about how much I could give, how well I could serve. I morphed from a go-getter into a go-giver! And I had the perfect laboratory. Remember the unrealistic, ice-cold boss? He vanished. I went to the office with a singular goal: *How can I best serve my staff and give them the tools they need to self-actualize?* If I missed the mark by even the tiniest bit, I reflected on how I could do better before I closed my eyes. No judgment, no self-abuse, no negative self-talk.

In the morning, I woke to meditation, thanking God for my sobriety first and foremost. But it was also a time to look forward into my day, to prepare myself for any stressors that could potentially come my way. I might think about a big meeting and the possibilities of what could happen so as to not be caught off guard. Even if I miscalculated and ended up with something I didn't plan for, my catchall hourly popup came to the rescue. Slowly, the way I responded to stress began to change.

Metaphorically speaking, I erected a wall of safety around me by soliciting co-conspirators in my sobriety. My wife and family were the first ones, of course, but also the Vision Dynamics staff protected me from my old world. It wasn't like my decision to try sobriety caused my phone to stop ringing. I was a good paying customer, and my drug connection was a businessman in his own right. But I created a world where he could no longer pitch his wares by first changing my personal phone numbers. Second, anyone who answered the phone at Vision Dynamics became instant detectives; they asked who was calling and from what company. If it smelled even a little fishy, they took messages.

By being disciplined and sticking to the plan, I could feel myself getting stronger. Then out of the blue I got an e-mail that would change my life forever.

CHAPTER 35

Who knows what circumstances conspired for that e-mail to appear in my inbox. I'd visited hundreds of websites, signed up for numerous online subscriptions, and purchased books, cassette tapes, and CDs, hunting for anything I could get my hands on to bolster my twelve-step program. Being sober wasn't enough for me.

I imagine that sounds a little awkward at this point. You might be thinking, *You friggin' idiot, you're lucky to even be alive. What do you mean, being sober wasn't enough?*

It simply wasn't. I had a nagging in my gut that I was supposed to be doing something. Once again there was something eating at me, but I wasn't quite sure what it was. Perhaps given my history, I should take a moment and clear the air. I had lots of clarity around the vodka bottle, but nevertheless something was calling me; I just knew it. Maybe you've had this notion before. Something, some idea, nudges you, but you're not quite sure what it is. It's as if someone's screamed your name in a stadium filled with people. You stop, stretch your ears as far as they will go, and search the crowd for a familiar face, a connection. Is this not the nature of callings? An unexpected tap on the shoulder that wakes to you a vision of who you could be. Maybe it's an idea so much bigger than you imagine yourself, and you might think, *Who, me? You're calling me? Fate, you can't be calling little ol' me.* You might even plug your ears in fear, hoping the calling will go away, but it doesn't. It turns into the type of nagging I began to feel, a pin-prickling kind of restlessness that made me question. It got to the point where I'd come home after a day at the office, plop in my easy chair, and think, *This can't be all there is.*

Then, as it always does, when we are ready and open, the universe provides. I recall the title of the e-mail saying something about self-esteem, so I clicked on it.

It was an e-mail from Jack Canfield. Now, before I tell you the story, let me set the table. I had no idea the world of personal development even existed. The idea that one could reach higher spiritual planes was completely foreign to me. I knew about religion, yes: go to Mass, pray, say some Hail Mary's, try to be a better person during the week, confess. Then do it all over again the next Sunday.

However, this notion that I could take an intentional journey inside to examine my thought processes was new to me. When I began to consider the possibilities, I had a conversation with myself that went something like this.

"Wait, hold up a second. You mean I can slow down and take a look at my thoughts?"

Yes, you can.

"And you're saying there is a chance that everything I ever thought was wrong?"

Highly possible...

"But I can do something about it?"

Oh, yeah.

"Really?"

Of course you can. All you have to do is do it.

Remember the scene when I destroyed my basement? Well, this revelation was the inverse: it was a shower of nutrients, vitamins, and minerals in perfect measurements. It was all that I'd been missing, all that I'd ever needed. It was photosynthesis causing me to stretch out toward the sun. It was a new birth. And I will admit, it has become a new addiction.

The details of the e-mail escape me at this point. What I do recall, however, is a feeling that somebody was inside my head. The contents hit a bull's-eye, speaking directly to what I still perceived as "my suffering," so I purchased a set of CDs.

The day they arrived, I rushed to my home office and popped in the first one, prepared to learn. I had my notebook and my fat-tipped black Sharpie; I was ready. From the first words there was downshifting of gears, a gigantic exhale, a calmness that I was in the right place and doing the right thing. Sobriety had, for the most part, eliminated the mania that had made up my thought process: that frantic, fly-like buzzing from one idea to the next, gobbling life as if there was no tomorrow. I had slowed down and was getting things done with efficiency. But this was deeper, a settling—intuitive confidence, if you will. I was pretty sure this was what had called me from the crowd.

The CD began with the concept of victimization. It looked at the notion of human behavior and our propensity to blame outside sources for our woes. At some point the question was posed: *Have you ever thought, "Why does this keep happening to me?"* As one of the world's best rationalizers, top-notch complainers, and superstar blamers of all time, I'd asked myself that question two hundred thousand times, maybe more. So you can imagine how hard a concept like "You alone are responsible for all your problems" hit me. It was a left hook on the chin, an algebraic equation with a difficulty factor of a thousand, yet it had the color of eternal wisdom at the same time. I smelled the truth but couldn't quite wrap my brain around the idea. "What a bunch of crap," I mumbled. But I was so intrigued that I kept listening. And then I listened again and again. Every session, a little more of the onion skin peeled away, and the sun of "I am responsible" rose in my life. That was a humungous deal.

All my life I had blamed my eyes, felt sorry for myself, and walked around with feelings of inferiority. Jack Canfield, via his CD, began to erode those crutches as a gentle stream carves its path through stone. He would later blow them to smithereens publicly, at one of his seminars.

Now I'm hooked; I was a CD junkie. Every time I listened, I grew a little more. The ah-ha moments came in wave after wave. My life was rounding into shape; I was becoming that vision of myself that I'd always held. My relationships were healing, my company was back on track, I felt strong, and I was sober. I said to myself, *If Jack Canfield is this transformative on CD, what might he do if I saw him in person?* I had to find out.

By the time I arrived in San Diego, I held an unshakable brand of happy that stems from knowing big things are on the horizon. I was going to see Jack Canfield, Mr. *Chicken Soup for the Soul*, live! This man's principles and ideas had been the completion of the puzzle that was my life. They were a perfect partnership to my twelve-step program. Together, they wove a fabric that I would go so far as to call moral—my very own commandments. That being said, I offer two concepts that set the foundation for my daily living; I'll share them with you before I talk about the experience at my first seminar, because I'd been practicing them like I was preparing for the Super Bowl.

Jack Canfield co-authored a book called *The Aladdin Factor*. It's an amazing book and a must-read. The book centers on the idea that you can't receive what you want unless you ask for it. A novel concept, right? Asking for what you want? Seems logical enough. But do you *really* ask for what you want? Do you even know how? Before I read it, I would have said yes to all the above. Pretty quickly, however, I realized I didn't know very much about asking. In fact, I was the poster boy for all five of the reasons people fail to ask for what they want.

The first was ignorance. People simply don't know what to ask for. It seems most of us don't take the time to stop and think about what it is we really want. Well, I was guilty as charged.

The second was limiting and inaccurate beliefs—negative self-images that have been subconsciously programmed into our minds. Think about my life as I've described it. Again, guilty.

The third reason people failed to ask was fear. Do I even need to say anything about that?

The fourth was low self-esteem. Most people don't feel worthy of the finer things in life. My self-esteem has been well documented in this chronicle.

The fifth and final reason was pride. Most people feel that by asking for help, they are admitting a weakness. There was no way on earth I could ever admit that I was weak. No way. With *The Aladdin Factor* under my belt, I began perfecting the art of asking. I remain a work in progress.

However, of all the principles that I've adopted over the years, "E + R = O" is the one I turn too most often. The Events in our lives, plus our Response, equals our Outcomes. In fact, it is a concept that I teach to my audiences. Most have heard it said in some form or another; it has been expounded upon by great sages from Buddha to Krishna to Jesus and most recently in *The Secret*. It's not what happens to us; rather, it is how we react that creates our world.

There I was in San Diego. I'd been working and I was ready to play with the big boys. Well, my wheels begin to wobble on the first day; by day two they were shaking and ready to fall off. Then Jack Canfield stepped in and did something that changed everything, and it ultimately brought you here to read my life's journey.

CHAPTER 36

I use a fat-tipped black Sharpie when I write because it creates thick lines that, when contrasted against the white background of paper, make reading much easier. I can actually read my writing without the use of a device. You might mistake it as third-grade scribble—huge, printed letters that aren't the most aesthetic in the world—but they work for me.

That's what I was doing when my newfound principles faced their first test. I was at Jack Canfield's seminar writing like a madman with my Sharpie. He was live on stage, and I was having a virtual out-of-body experience. I was tingling. I mean, he was good on CD, but in person? He was Jerry Garcia live at Madison Square Garden. My endorphins were pinging, and I nodded in agreement. I should also add this was my first time in San Diego. If you never been there, put it on your list, because the city is stunning. King and queen palm trees, miles of beaches, and perfect sun without the humidity.

Quite naturally I was thinking, *This is the best thing that's ever happened to me.* Then, abruptly the woman sitting next to me gives me a gentle elbow. I thought I might have been a little too close, so I scooted over, never lifting my pen. She nudged me again, this time a little harder. I pried my eyes away from the stage and asked, "Yes?" I thought, *What on earth could be so important?*

She said, "Would you mind using something else?"

Maybe it was the confused look on my face, because before I ask what on earth she was talking about, she said, "Your pen smells really bad. It's bothering me."

Like I told you, I'd been practicing. And like magic I was presented with a chance to put my work into action. One of the many revelations born out of *The Aladdin Factor* was the importance of *my* needs, the idea that Charlie Collins's wants and desires were just as important as anyone's in the universe. That included doctors, lawyers, CEOs, and even the woman sitting next to me. This was my chance to reply, "I'm sorry the smell bothers you, but I have a vision disorder. It's a long story, but I need to use this particular pen. Let's find a compromise." But instead, I put the Sharpie away and took out a ballpoint, knowing I would never be able to read my notes. Resentful, it was the first dent in my armor.

Day two came along, and I was awake early because I was fired up. Other than Sharpie-gate, the first day was more than I could have expected. During one of the breaks, I had a chance to personally meet Jack and shake his hand. As always, he was gracious, warm, and genuinely appreciative of my attendance. Awestruck may not be a strong enough word for me. He was a hero figure, and I'm sure I blushed. In my mind day two was going to be even better. I got something to eat and headed over to the meeting room early so that I could get a front-row seat.

When I arrived, the attendant was all smiles and said, "Good morning. Please pick up your name tag from the table, and then you can head inside."

I felt a jolt of nerves, and my legs filled with wet cement. I glanced around the room thinking, *Oh crap!* Nametags on a table could be problematic. No one at the seminar knew I was legally blind because I'd been hiding it.

I made me way over to the table, nonchalantly scanned the room, and quickly bent over the table... I got my face as close to the badges as possible, but I couldn't find my name; the print was too small. My nerves began to fray. In the background I could hear attendees arriving. Their voices were filled with the excitement that I'd had only moments before. My old companion fear had come out of thin air and wrapped his fingers around my neck; he was squeezing, and my heart began to race. *They're gonna know. They're gonna find out I'm a defect. I can't hide it.* I started to feel sorry for myself. *Maybe you don't belong here. These people are doctors, lawyers, and CEOs. They're smart. You can't even find your badge, loser!*

Recalling the moment causes me to shake my head in disbelief. It's hard to imagine that after all I'd overcome, a feeling of inferiority could still grip me so tightly and so quickly, but it did. I decided it might be better if I went back to my room. I didn't belong and wasn't good enough. I'd just sit in my room with the blinds drawn, watching *Judge Judy* or *The Price Is Right*. If anyone even noticed I was missing and bothered to ask where I was, I'd tell them I got sick.

With shoulders slumped, I turned away from the table and headed for my room. I was closing in on the door when I thought, *No! I'm not going to run. I'm going to ask for help.*

I made it back to the table, and there was a woman standing there searching for her badge. "Excuse me," I said. "Would you mind helping me find my name tag? I have a vision problem, and I can't read the print."

She smiled. "Of course. What's your name?" She handed me my badge and went about her business of enjoying Jack Canfield's seminar. She had no idea how that passing incident would affect my life in such a profound way.

As the universe would have it, the first session of day two covered the topic of asking. I sat there wondering, *How could this be? He's got hidden cameras in the building.* He was back inside my head and dissecting my morning event at the table. It was so freaky that I was compelled to share the story with him during the break. I gave him the Cliff's Notes version of my life and capped it with the morning badge incident. Jack congratulated me on breaking through a barrier, and I was proud of myself. I'd made progress and thought it was done.

When the session resumed, the first thing out of Jack's mouth was, "Can you please bring the microphone up here to Charlie?"

I sat straight up. *Did he just say Charlie?* I used what little vision I had to peer at the stage, and it looked like he was pointing my general direction. I took a nervous glance over my shoulder, thinking, *Oh my God, there'd better be someone else named Charlie.* But the seas parted, and I felt the action was coming my way. My heart broke down the barn door and took off racing like a wild horse. *They'd better not be handing me that mic...* Remember the kid that told the teacher, "Just give me an F?" He showed up. *I'm not good enough to talk in front of three hundred people of this caliber!* At that point, all I'd ever spoken to was room full of little old ladies who reminded me of my grandmother. This was different; these people were smart. But to my dismay, the mic ended up in my hand.

"Charlie," Jack said, "would you mind standing up?"

I got to my feet shaking so badly that I swore the people around me could hear my knees knocking.

Jack said to the audience, "Charlie came up to me at the break and told me an interesting story." Then he said to me, "Charlie, I'd like for you to share that same story with the group."

I did. I told a room full of people whom I'd never met the quick story about my life as best I could, because I was extremely nervous. "I'm legally blind," I said. "I've always felt less than... Couldn't see my badge... I thought I shouldn't be here..."

When I finished, Jack asked, "How long have you been doing that—this thinking that's been giving you the results in your life?"

"Well, all my life, really."

"And how's that working for you?"

"Not too good," I admitted.

"No, it isn't," he agreed before pausing to gather his words. "And let's see if I've got this right. Because you have legal blindness, you feel less than, like you're not smart enough. The reality is you've basically taken something that affects eyes and given it power over your whole body. It's controlling your entire life."

I'd never thought of it in those terms, but he was right.

"By a show of hands," he said, "how many people in this room would have helped him, if Charlie had asked?"

First hands went up, and then people started clapping.

"Charlie, do you understand what humans are on this earth to do? We are here to serve. We're here to give to each other, to bring value, and to make a difference."

Keep in mind I was near the front row and standing. Behind me was a room filled with the smartest people I'd ever been around.

Then Jack asked pointedly, "How are you ever going to allow that to happen? How do you expect to receive help and be served—or on the other hand, be able to help someone else—when you're only thinking of yourself and your problems?"

The hair on my neck stood up. It felt like the room suddenly went dark, and the brightest spotlight beamed only on me. I thought, *Who does this guy think he is, calling me out in front of these people?*

True, I was embarrassed by having my crutches kicked out from under me so publicly. But the audience didn't see it that way—they were cheering. It took just a moment to realize they were cheering *for* me. Their offer of support was the catalyst for what stands as the transformative moment in my life, the lifting of the veil, the moment I set foot on the path of ultimate healing. There I was, legally blind and stripped naked for the world to see. And guess what? They liked me. They didn't give a rip that I was legally blind. I didn't need to be anything other than just me.

When the day was done, Jack pulled me aside. "I hope that was okay," he said. "I only did it because I feel you are ready to go to the next level in life. And that's what you call coaching."

That's what you call coaching, I repeated silently. A bell had gone off. I grew very still, sinking deeper into my skin with a rising smile. From what I could tell, I had met my mentor. After a long, arduous journey, in five mundane words he explained who I was. I was a coach. Charlie "Padre" Collins had always been a coach. Misguided? Yes, of course. But I was indeed a coach.

In that moment, standing before Jack Canfield, I was born into who I am today.

CHAPTER 37

Life-changing event.

That's the best I can do: offer up a pallid attempt to explain the transformation at my first Jack Canfield seminar. In all honesty, though, nothing I write would even come close to truly revealing what happened. At best, I present an art deco mansion painted in bland eggshell white; a circus without the flying trapeze; an orchestra sans violins. I realize assigning words to the workings of the soul is the business of experts; writers like Maya Angelou or Henry David Thoreau come to mind. If you don't mind, I'll stay in my lane and tell you in plain old English: I went back to Connecticut a changed man.

Before I took off, however, I decided to sign up for Jack's next event, called *Breakthrough to Success*. I recalled it being billed as seven days of intensive, hands-on, interactive workshops. It was going to take what I had learned in San Diego to the next level—still a little scary for yours truly, but there was no turning back. Plus, it was about six months away, giving me plenty of time to work on my personal development.

I landed in Connecticut and hit the ground running. Remember when I talked about drugs penetrating every aspect of my life, and everything being bad? Well, the coin got flipped, and everything was good. I had a formula, a plan. I approached life with deliberate intention on being a better husband, father, son, brother, and leader. I ate clean, healthy food. I got plenty of exercise. I dove deeper into my twelve-step program and chomped down on personal development with an iron jaw. Jack Canfield helped me to see the tiniest glimpse of my future, and I wanted it badly. I started by devouring his entire catalogue; I read everything he had in print.

I picked up other authors as well, but there was something about Jack's delivery that struck the tuning fork inside me. I'm sure you know this feeling, when someone's words hit you just right. You've heard it before, but not quite in the same way. With that on the table, let me make a quick point.

This knowledge flows from an eternal wellspring, from One God Source, and it's been here since the foundations of the Earth. If you took it upon yourself to study the great religions and the works of the great sages, and you toss in the so-called new age movement, you would find them more similar than different, because they all boil down to one word: love. They're about finding that path to first love the person in the mirror and then extending that love to all living things. So I suggest to you, my fellow seeker, to keep reading and keep digging, and when you find that right voice, study and practice. That is what I did. I continued to work with the staples I spoke of earlier. I evoked the principles of asking for what I wanted and taking 100 percent responsibility for the outcomes in my life—not 99 percent but 100 percent. I could feel myself growing steady by the day. It was beyond freeing.

Now for the good part.

I'm often asked, "How will I know when I've found my calling?"

My reply is always the same. "You won't find it—you'll discover it. And trust me, you'll know when it happens."

There is a grounding that comes along with being in harmony that's unmistakable. It's like your foundation suddenly roots as an unshakable, great oak. You see the future in your mind's eye and embrace it. The tap on the shoulder offering a vision that may have been a little scary? Well, it's still scary, but you move on anyway. You can't help it; the power pushing you toward a vision of self is too strong. I saw my future. I saw myself on stage helping, teaching, sharing my story with those who needed to hear it.

By the way, that giant that once sat on my shoulder telling me I was a loser? It turned out he was a midget. And when he did attempt to open his squeaky little voice, he got buried in a barrage of affirmations.

On my other shoulder now sat a cheerleader, and he had a bullhorn on repeat, blasting declarations of truth not aimed at some distant point in the future but in the now. He spoke them, and I wrote them down. I have notebooks filled with the following:

- *I am a public speaker helping people to see again.*
- *I am Charlie Collins, a master at teaching people how to see again.*
- *I am a winner.*
- *I am a champion.*

This wasn't ego or false bravado like before. I was simply very sure of where I was going and why. I had come to learn that sighted people suffer from blindness, too—the inability to *see* happens in the brain. It turned out my blindness had been a gift. Not only could I help those with blindness related to vision loss, but I could help those living in darkness of other kinds. The seeds had already been planted. What little public speaking I had done almost always elicited two comments: "You're a great speaker. You should do more of that." Or, "You should write a book." I finally believed it and was taking baby steps toward my destiny.

Six months passed, and I hopped on a flight to Arizona. It was August, and the heat was otherworldly. The air engulfed me in a big, sweaty bear hug when I stepped out of the airport. I had never in my life felt anything close. But it turned out to be a good thing. Serendipitous. Because of the heat, I landed in a gigantic suite for next to nothing. It was so cheap that I had to ask why—I felt there had to be a catch. "It's August in Arizona, sir," was the answer I got.

I strolled into the seminar on day one ready to rock and roll. The anticipation was something I'll never forget. I didn't have butterflies—it was a hornet's nest.

Right off I was greeted by attendants who remembered me from the San Diego event. They welcomed me like an old friend and ushered me to a front-row seat. *Okay, this is a nice touch,* I thought. I felt important, like a celebrity.

The first day was fantastic. I witnessed, live and in color, one of the great teachers of our time, and he was on top of his game, even better than before. It felt like he was speaking directly to me. In my defense, I still hadn't learned that my problems, for lack of better words, were of the garden variety. My frustrations were no different than the next man's. But I was hanging on to the last threads of "Nobody knows pain like I do. My eyes are bad."

At some point during the day, Jack announced that two attendees would be chosen to take the stage on Friday; they would be given a chance to deliver a three-minute presentation to inspire the group. He said, "If you're interested, write down on a note card why I should put you on stage. Thursday will be the last day to turn it in."

The last part got away from me because as soon as he said, "Get up on stage," I entered into knockdown, drag-out, internal dialogue.

This is it! Here we go, baby!

"There's no way I'm getting up in front of all these smart people. You must be nuts!"

But this is who you are! What's the problem?

"I can't. I'm not ready."

Yes, you are. This is our—

"He'll never pick me anyway."

The seminar was better than advertised. It was intense, requiring every ounce of presence I could muster. We did some big-time digging in the breakout groups, and at times I felt extremely vulnerable. But I must say that the second there was a break in the action, my thoughts drifted to being on that stage. I thought about Friday with excitement and fear. I wanted so badly to be chosen, but I was scared to death at the same time. I prepared anyway.

In fact, I started Monday night. While everyone else hit the town, I went back to my room, reworked my notes, and started practicing. This was where Arizona heat did me a solid. The suite was so big that I was able to move exactly how I would on stage. I walked from side to side, visualizing being on stage. I used a pencil as a microphone and worked the room. "Hi, my name is Charlie Collins, and I'm president and founder of Vision Dynamics."

Here's a piece of valuable information. If you want something, you have to first believe you can have it, and then you have to visualize yourself doing it. Then you must prepare for the moment. So that's what I did. Even in the midst of the internal turmoil about being on stage I practiced; during lunch breaks and at night. Whenever time permitted, I would hustle to my room, grab the pencil, and start working the room. During the seminar I imagined I was Jack. *Looks easy enough to me,* one side of me would say. *All he's doing is walking back and forth across the stage and talking. You can do that.*

Then the naysayer would chime in. *Are you out of your mind? That's Jack Canfield! You could never do that.* And so the internal battle raged.

CHAPTER 38

By the time Thursday rolled around, I was a giant bundle of nerves. The workshop, on the one hand, had been the experience of a lifetime. I laughed, cried, shared, and bonded deeply with others. But all the while, I'd had one eye on Friday. It was coming, closing in like an armada of battleships on the horizon. Now they'd landed on my beach, and I had to do something. The problem was that I couldn't find peace either way. Half of me yearned to be chosen. The other half wanted to bolt for the bathroom stall, put my feet up on the toilet, and hold my breath. I was torn down the middle, sitting in my chair during the opening remarks.

That was where I was mentally when Jack reminded us, "Noon is the cutoff time to submit your note cards, if you want to be considered for a presentation."

I began to fidget and felt heat rising off my skin as the internal shouting match kicked in full force.

Go for it!

"I can't! I just can't. Not in front of all these smart people."

But we've been practicing since Monday. We're ready.

"No, we're not…"

At ten o'clock, the first break came and went. I did nothing except worry.

By noon I was incredibly antsy, so much so that I began to wonder if anyone in my breakout group noticed the stress. My ability to concentrate on the work faded. All I could think about was being on stage—or not. I was going for it. Then I wasn't. Then I was.

You're probably thinking, *Dude, can you just make a decision and spare all the drama?*

Have mercy on me, please. And remember you're only reading about the turmoil. Imagine what it was like in real time! My armpits were sweating. My heart was racing. My gut was twisting into fast knots.

Lunch arrived and I picked over my food, ultimately concluding a big opportunity was about to pass.

You're not going be picked anyway. Why not just turn something in? You could at least say you tried.

Just as lunch was ending, I ripped a half-sheet of paper out of my notebook; a note card would have never worked because I couldn't write that small. And that was perfect in my mind. Jack was such a stickler about following directions that I figured I would never be picked, even though that's what I really wanted.

I quickly wrote something that might have read like this:

Dear Jack,

My name is Charlie Collins. I believe my life story and the struggles I've overcome could be an inspiration to the program participants... blah... blah... blah...

Then, believe it or not, I had to talk myself into getting out of the seat to turn it in! I started and then stopped. Started, then stopped. Had you been watching, I'm sure it played as pure keystone comedy. I inched up to the stack like it was a roaring blaze, turning my head to avoid the heat. I tossed my entry, looked around, and then bolted as if I'd robbed a bank.

On Friday morning, the jitters jumped all over me the second my eyes opened. I sat straight up in bed thinking, *I can't see how I'll be selected. There's no way. There are some big-time heavy hitters in the group. CEOs, lawyers, doctors, professors, writers ... and me. Why would I be chosen? I'm just a blind guy trying to make sense of the world.*

I got myself together and made my way to the session.

We go through the morning work, while my insides twisted and turned. Finally the moment of truth arrived. Jack called the first name, and I'm both disappointed and relieved. The guy takes the stage and knocks it clean out of the park. He uses inflection, his diction is flawless, and he covers the stage, using his hands like a pro. *Wait a second,* I thought. *He's a pro. No fair!*

And his story? Oh my God, was it compelling. He wove a dramatic tale of dead-end alcohol abuse and how it caused him to lose everything— his wife, his kids, his friends, his business. He told of sitting in his den in a pile of empty gin bottles, the tip of a butcher's knife pressed against his sternum. Life was over. He was going to end it all... It was only after he finished that I realized I was holding my breath.

The first thing I thought was, *Charlie, you idiot! How are you gonna follow that? How stupid. Good thing Jack's never going to call your name. You'd better hope he doesn't...*

I hadn't finished my thoughts when I heard, "Our next presenter will be Charlie Collins."

I completely iced over—deer in the headlights. I couldn't move.

The woman sitting next to me said, "He just called your name," and gave me an elbow. She had a huge grin on her face, and this was what flashed in my mind. Our group had been working with a set of tools to control fear. I'm was sure her smile was saying, *Go on. Let me see what you've got, big boy.*

Of course I tried, but fear overran my walls like troops storming a castle. There's only one other time my body behaved the way it did when I tried to stand. I was out on my boat, and gale-force winds swooped down out of nowhere, tossing and spinning me like a wine cork in a hot tub. I honestly I thought I was going to die. I struggled, fought, used every ounce of my energy to finally dock safely. As soon as my legs touched dry land, I began to shake violently and then collapsed. This feeling was what I felt coming on, so I started a fast conversation with myself. *You are going to look like a real idiot if you pass out before you make it to the stage. Calm down.*

I don't even recall walking; it was like I blinked, and suddenly I was listening to the guy attaching the microphone to my shirt. I was clearly nervous. "You're gonna do fine," he said. "He wouldn't have picked you if he didn't think you were ready."

Whatever, pal.

Now I was all wired up and ready to go. But before I got started, Jack laid down some rules. "You are not allowed to start by saying, 'I'm nervous. I've never done this before.' None of that business. Get right into your presentation."

My jaw hit the floor. *Are you kidding me?* I thought. *He just took away my opening.*

Five, four, three, two, one. He gave me the green light, and there I was in my moment of truth. The kid who'd said, "Just fail me," was on stage in front of four-hundred people at a Jack Canfield seminar.

Jack himself was standing in the wings, watching.

I know you're dying to know if I choked. Guess what? I didn't. Four days of preparation kicked in, and I took off. I'd already spoke to this audience in my mind a bunch of times. I'd already walked across the stage in my mind. And I'd watched Jack like a hawk, or a low-vision hawk, at least. I knew what excellence looked like, and I went about imitating him.

If you offered me a hundred thousand dollars, I couldn't tell you what I said. Something took over me, and I found that space athletes call the zone. I was right there in the moment—no past, no future, just right there. Then suddenly the room erupted in laughter. I was surprised wondering what could be so funny. I mean, I wasn't intending to crack jokes; I was just being Charlie. Moments later the room burst into full-blown laughter for the second time.

Now I was feeling it, and I was comfortable. I settled into my calling like a pair of custom, handmade shoes. I worked the stage just like I did in my room. People were laughing, and I was as happy as I'd ever been.

When I finished, the crowd jumped to their feet and gave me a standing ovation. Four-hundred people applauding me. *Me!*

Can you comprehend the emotional flood washing over the little boy who believed, for his entire life, that he was less than? It was celestial, reminiscent of the white peace I felt being near death after my train accident. Maybe they clapped for ten seconds; perhaps it was thirty seconds. Whatever it was, I stood there soaking in the energy through my cells. My self-esteem soared so stratospherically high that it would never come down. It was, without question, the moment of my true birth.

Jack congratulated me on a job well done, and it was time for me to leave the stage. Ever the prankster, I decided to have a little fun, considering that everyone now knew I was legally blind.

When I was unhooked from the microphone, I made a beeline for the front of the stage. When I reached the edge, I pitched forward and flailed my arms. I heard the collective gasp of the room; the table just under me started scrambling. Arms flew in the air to catch the poor blind guy who couldn't see where he was going.

When the panic reached its height, I stood tall, pointed, and said, "Gotcha!"

I was ready to begin my life in earnest. I turned and floated off the stage on the wings of a standing ovation. I've never looked back.

Charlie Collins is the Founder and CEO of both Vision Dynamics and CCI (Charlie Collins International). He is a well-respected Transformational Professional Speaker, Certified Professional Success Coach, and author who inspires people to live with clear vision.

Legally blind since age 13, Charlie struggled with accepting his vision loss and understands the pitfalls of low self-esteem. His "Tripping Into The Light" seminars, based upon real life challenges, offer participants a sense of hope by teaching how to create clear, attainable visions of success.

Charlie lives in Connecticut with his wife and two daughters. In his spare time he loves to play the guitar, ride his mountain bike and go on hikes, but most of all he enjoys spending time with his family and friends.

For more information, visit:
www.TrippingintotheLight.com
www.CharlieCollinsInternational.com

CPSIA information can be obtained at www.ICGtesting.com
Printed in the USA
BVOW07s1859270814

364543BV00002B/10/P